LAUGHTER OF
THE STONES

by

Lee Lozowick

HOHM PRESS
Tabor, N.J.

published by

HOHM PRESS
P.O. Box 75
Tabor, NJ
07878

Printed in the U.S.A.   ISBN: 0-934252-00-9

Preface

How To Read This Book — A Short Note

Part I of this volume might seem to the casual reader like a delightfully new and refreshing series of meditations, daily inspirations, or affirmations. But they should not be taken so lightly as to be read once, laughed over, or relegated to the depths of profundity and then promptly forgotten.

Each "moment of truth" is not what it may seem, not as shallow as its own language, and not as obvious as first impressions may make it appear. If the reader would like to be embraced, as has the author, he or she should use this tome as a study manual or guide. Each statement in itself is a world, even a universe that could possibly take years to fully grasp. Do not debase the statements by using them as mere affirmations, but see them as a mystical revelation about your life. Each "moment" should be taken as a deeply personal expression of your being.

Very much as the proverbial oak tree from a small acorn grows, so too can a dawning of light explode as a nova star from a small droplet of sun. And such is each "moment" that droplet of sun.

So do not relegate this book to the dusty recesses of your library after a cursory reading. The questions involved often take time to sort out, to place properly, and simply to mature in experience once they have been planted in consciousness. Read the book once, perhaps twice, let it rest for a month, and then read it again. After doing so, let yourself intuitively select those "moments" which are most personal for you. Study in a mood of openness and vulnerability, so that you will most assuredly derive the greatest benefit possible.

Part II may also need a bit of explanation. Again, upon

superficial observation, the short essays may appear to be humorous, or satirical, or even in certain cases, an attack on traditions or conventions. Experience may indicate that, on an outer level, comedy and theatrical satire is often quite entertaining, and certainly, in the light mood it creates, enjoyable.

If the reader reflects a little more deeply however, he or she might see that there is a great seriousness beneath most comedy, and an absolutely relevant social or socio-political message beneath most satire. The lightness of the delivery simply serves to mask the crucial need to become more "human" human beings.

At the same time, Part II may at times seem critical, challenging, or even highly cynical. Yet, the cynic is often a truly compassionate being. He does not know how to socially communicate, so frustratedly cries out to mankind through the antagonism and bitterness of his cynicism.

Therefore, it is important that each essay be read with a clear eye and a childlike, wondering heart. Do not let the message of the need to be Real and Alive be obscured by threats to your established attitudes and approaches to your own spiritual life. For before one can be Real, he must, of necessity, realize his unrealness. Each of the probing and oftimes surgical essays attempts to do just that. Each one cuts through a level of learned (and very protective) sophistication, exposing a core that is more raw, less known or sure, yet infinitely Truer.

It has been the author's experience that each essay is a most effective tool in this process, acting literally as an awakener that can rouse the slumbering giant of spirituality within each individual. Do not, for your own sake, shrug Part II off too lightly.

And last, but by no means least, enjoy to your heart's content.

Amen

Table of Contents

Photo Credits:
Courtesy of Paul Peckham
Pages - 4, 6, 12, 16, 24, 26, 34, 50.

Courtesy collection of Adele Lozowick
Pages - 8, 14, 20, 22, 28, 30, 32, 38, 42, 44, 48, 52, 54, 56.

Part I

"Just this."
"Just what?"
"This!"
"This what?"
"Oh, just this."

If you think back to when you were a kid, remember what was important to you. Maybe when you were five, what was really important to you was the kindergarten Halloween party where you went to school with your costume on. Or as parents, your kids may say to you, "I've got to have this air hockey game. I really want it." And you know in a month, they are even going to play with it. But it is so important to them now.

We all have these things as kids that are crucial to us. They really are, as far as we are concerned. They are absolutely important.

Well, adults are exactly the same as kids. Whatever you think is important now is no more important than what you thought was important as a kid. Right now, it is really important, and a month or a year from now, it will be forgotten. The thing of true importance is the One who never changes: God.

Life is our playground. We shouldn't look outside and say, "Oh, rain another day?" Simply go out and play in the rain. Just don't complain if something gets ruined when it gets wet.

In the beginning was the Word, and the Word was with God. What happened after there was the Word? The Word made the world. Not God. God created the Word and the Word created the world. The Word is mind.

There's no easy way out.

Being psychic or using siddhis isn't silly or stupid necessarily — simply frivolous.

Anyone who has ever "gotten it" by following some so-called method, has gotten it in spite of the method, not because of it.

Spiritual life is very passionate, not some dry heady dissertation on the absolute. It is life overflowing with juice and energy.

The clue to Spiritual Work is not to run in place; it is to be in place.

The only way one ever learns that he or she is perfectly all right is to be all right in front of everybody. When one is all right in front of everybody it will start to dawn on him that he really is all right after all.

Real consciousness is beneath all activity. All of the, "Now, I'm angry, now I'm happy, etc." is just another form of analysis. All "self-remembering" or self-observation is, by its nature, anaytical, and therefore separative. For who is there to analyze? Even saying, "Always remember God" is false, for there is not one to remember. If one knows or sees that he or she is conscious, it is false. Who is there to know?

Changing the World
1. Establish Your Own Health
   and Happiness Through Ma[thema]tics
2. Understanding of What [...]
3. Change Orientation of [...]
   a. $Na^+ \longrightarrow K[...]$

The first thing to do in beginning Spiritual Work is to actually possess what we think we possess.

Change comes through responsibility only, never through hope. For when one is responsible, he is not concerned about changing, but about being.

Because God is simply and always perfectly present, alive and joyous, there is eternally no "goal" that is ever reached.

Spiritual life is to be lived functionally in the world, but the assumptions upon which the world sustains its activity are not to be swallowed. This is to be in the world and not of it.

Our lives are founded on compromise. But the Divine is absolute, in which there can be no compromise. We cannot make a deal. We must either yield to the absolute or not play the game.

Seeking relief *is* suffering, not a way to eliminate it.

If you were to wake up tomorrow morning, that would really be nice. If you don't wake up tomorrow morning, have a good sleep.

We must always start at the beginning. Not very profound but definitely consistent with truth.

Spiritual practice is to a) establish discipline   b) refine perception to enable one to realize with less psychic interference, c) to point out, by its own nature, the futility of spiritual practice bringing one to live God   d) none of the above.

Never give an answer to more than what is being asked.

We are always being asked to act. The degree to which we can act consciously is the degree to which we are free.

The ego can't be reasoned with. One can't sit down with it and say, "Don't you see that it's all suffering?" or, "Wouldn't you be happier if you realized God?" The ego simply will not respond to reason. Fortunately, it can be tricked. Perfect devotees are always being tricked into being perfect devotees.

If you are sitting home alone in your room, you think you are lonely because you don't have a friend to go out with, or because there isn't a good movie playing. You always think you wouldn't be lonely if . . . It's when you are in the middle of doing the thing you thought would make it all right, and you still feel just as lonely that you begin to see that only God satisfies.

Ego is the freedom of the mind selecting an alternative to God

The logic of the mind is totally illogical.

Understanding the Dharma doesn't matter if, by chance, the Enlightened One sits next to you at the ice cream parlor eating His chocolate sundae, and you don't recognize Him.

If one says he has seen the frustration of seeking, and is still frustrated, he hasn't seen it.

Heaven's not where you think it is.

There is a great process that has been labeled "God" by the religious traditions. The traditions have remained sterile forms of empty ritual, while the process continues in spite of its crusaders. Don't we intuitively know that "life goes on"?

We are not who we think we are.

There is nothing inside of God; there is nothing outside of God. There is no relationship that takes place in terms of God. There is just God.

Trying to "get to God" is like trying to repair damage that has never been done. Isn't that absurd?

The principle of God is the ground in which activity is qualified.

As we look at one another, it is tacitly obvious that we are separate. I am sitting here. You are sitting there. Our sensory input demands us to see that we are not connected. Everything we have ever known, seen, heard and perceived has verified that. And yet, in Truth, we are not separate. That paradox itself is the dilemma of spiritual life.

There is no God to listen, no bliss or ecstasy to achieve. The Gift has already been given. One can either enjoy the Gift, or throw away the wrapping paper, stick the present in a closet, and start counting the days until next Christmas.

Agreement is just as bad as criticism. There is no need to agree or disagree. Just do.

Normal spiritual "highs", "samadhis", etc. are dependent for their very existence on whatever brought them about: practice, mantra, chakra, community, or whatever. True realization is not dependent. It just is, always, already perfect.

If one has to stop to meditate, he's missed the point.

This is the only reason we exist: To please God. Esotericism is a lie.

The only way anyone can have everything is to be nothing.

Real intelligence is understanding that you don't understand.

If we were meant to give up the world, either it or we wouldn't be here.

The only reason we are here is because it is God's Game. All the world is a game, and men and women merely pieces...Where have I heard that before?

If you desire the Grace of God, simply be willing to suffer the outrage of His play.

The spiritual student thinks that the more experience he has, the farther he has gotten. Actually, no matter how much he has experienced, he hasn't moved.

There are no such things as tests. There are only lessons.

The student sees the Guru's Play as arbitrary; the Guru sees His Play as spontaneous. It is the difference between living the life of suffering and living the life of God.

Awakening to God is often conceived of as a victory because of the illusion that there is something to attain, that there is a battle to be won. Actually, enlightenment is a defeat because all one does is become ordinary.

Healing has nothing to do with real spiritual life. Healing is healing and real spiritual life is sacrifice.

When one person awakens, the universe evolves another step.

Slavery to God is real independence. The lack of independence is being run by karmic destiny.

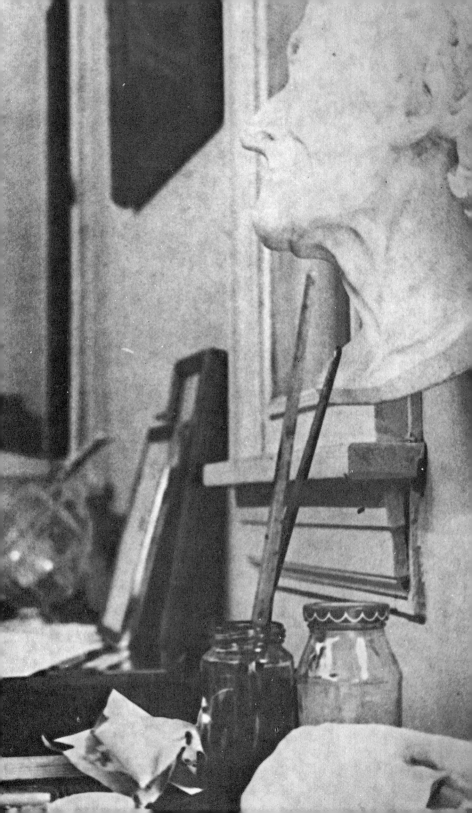

What one does for the Guru is the Guru's service to the doer. The more perfectly one is in relationship to the Guru, the more perfectly he is being served.

Devotion without humor is humorless.

The beginning stages of spiritual life don't progress until we stop taking things personally.

If one has only laughed with God, and never wept with Him, it isn't God that has been laughed with.

Two things are possible when it becomes clear that there is only God. One can become resigned to that fact, or one can celebrate. I choose to celebrate!

No matter what question the Guru is approached with, the answer is always the same: Love God.

The moment of awakening is just the beginning of Spiritual Work. Sorry to disappoint you.

When wonderful things are ordinary and ordinary things are wonderful, then at last God has been glimpsed.

It is only when one realizes he is nothing that he realizes that he is everything.

Who is a true martyr, the one who dies for a lost cause, or the one who dies because the cause has already been found?

Part II

Life In The Goldfish Bowl

One of my students gave me a "Nancy" comic the other day. Sluggo has a goldfish and he says, "What an awful life living in a little bowl. I'll give him his freedom." So sluggo takes the goldfish and he pours him into the lake. And then he doesn't need the goldfish bowl so he throws that into the lake too.

Well, the goldfish has got a big lake to enjoy, but he finds his bowl and swims inside it. And the last frame shows the goldfish in a gigantic lake in a universe of water living right in the little goldfish bowl where he always lived.

That's what people tend to do. The moment one sits with the Spiritual Master, that one is already free. Why? Because the Spiritual Master assumes it for the student. So you are already enlightened. You don't have to do anything. It's already done.

The Master sees the student swimming around in a little four foot pool, needing a little room, so he pours the student back into the lake. And when the student is in the middle of the lake, with no boundaries, he finds the goldfish bowl and again swims back inside. There he sits, free, looking out of the goldfish bowl, because that is where he has always been.

Now, there is a funny thing about swimming back into the bowl. When Sluggo had the fish, he would feed it every day. And the goldfish was very comfortable and very "happy". But after Sluggo threw the goldfish into the lake and he found his bowl again, he discovered that Sluggo was not going to feed him every day.

So what is he going to do? He is going to swim around the bowl every day getting very hungry, and he is going to say, "Where is my food?" He will swim around the bowl free, all the while being able to swim out to get food, wondering, "Where is my food? Gee, I was so happy and all of a sudden, I'm not happy anymore. I don't understand it."

It is the same in spiritual life. The student is in the goldfish bowl, and he isn't getting fed anymore. The world isn't doing it anymore. It no longer satisfies the way he knows he can be satisfied. He's got to get his own food because he is free. When he was not free, he could expect things to be done for him. He could expect his bowl to be cleaned out once in awhile. But when you are free, you can't expect that. The student has to do it himself. He is free. He has to swim out and find his own food. If he wants, just for old time sake, to go back and say, "Ah, there is my old bowl", he can do that. He can bring the Master by and say, "Hey look, there is my old bowl. I used to live there." And the Master will say, "You used to what? I don't understand. I was always free. You mean you weren't free?" And the student will say, "No". The Master won't understand because he is swimming around the lake.

And the student will say, "Well, you know, the search. . ." And the Master will say, "The search? What do you mean? Everything looks perfect to me. I don't see anything to be attained."

The student will say, "Yeah, but I'm not used to this big lake. There are big fish that could eat me up. I've got to be careful because I could get in trouble in this lake. I mean, there are fishermen. I've got to learn what hooks are and all this stuff." And the Master says, "I've been in this lake all my life. What are you talking about? You just swim along."

You see, the student doesn't have to learn the pitfalls and map the territory. He doesn't need to ask, "What if the Master asks me to give up my secret little pleasures? How am I going to earn a living? What about sex? What about insurance?" That is totally unnecessary. Just swim in the lake. After all, when your time is up, your time is up.

If you are swimming in the lake and a barracuda comes along, it is over in an instant. You don't even have time to be afraid. So why spend years and years worrying about barracudas when you've never even see one? You are already free. What are you worried about? Simply swim in the lake and get into your freedom.

The Divine Road Of Reactional Enquiry

For many years, eons, perhaps, a form of spiritual practice has been given to devotees by various Spiritual Masters. It has been spoken of in the ancient Vedic texts (Upanishads) and has been an aspect of various Buddhist cults as well. It has most recently been popularized by a very reknowned Indian sage. Each time this esoteric spiritual practice has been used it has been given in a form that has been most appropriate for the culture and the time in which it has arisen. Perhaps the most well known form of this technique is the statement "Who-Am-I?"

In case the reader may still by wondering what the technique is, it is called Enquiry. It is a process whereby the practitioner uses a word or series of words (called a statement) to turn in upon his or her consciousness. Ideally with the continued pursuit of this tested technique the practitioner can trace this consciousness all the way back to its source, which is the way it's supposed to work anyhow. The word or series of words (called a statement) is always in the form of a question which is either spoken (oral) or silent (thought). This question is directed in consciousness whenever an event arises that needs to be answered. Well, that may be a little unclear. Let's start over from the beginning (which is a very poor and all too prevalent habit that humans all tend to fall into).

In the beginning stages of Enquiring, the user (not to be confused with junkie, although occasionally the enquirer becomes a spiritual junkie, which is another story altogether so I won't cover it here!) must willfully create, direct and sustain the phrase (a series of words, otherwise known as a statement). This process is done at random moments in order to question the form of some experience that may be going on. It is used to serve the possibility of piercing insight into True Nature of the material, mental and emotional realms. When the false [which happens to be all experience that may be going on — so the technique can be used randomly and the user (not to be confused with — oh, never mind) never need worry about the technique being directed at something it shouldn't be. The user (not to be confused with — that's the problem with a habit, once it's in, it's a bitch to root out) shouldn't ever worry anyway which is another story altogether so I won't cover it here!] experience is questioned with the enquiring phrase or statement (a series of words otherwise known as a sentence or broken sentence) it eventually yields its falseness and superficiality to what is True and Real. The True and/or Real is always hidden within the false but is so obvious that it is never seen until the very last moment. It is so obvious, in fact, that it seems too simple and too pure to be true and since humans don't want to ever be "wrong" (not that they're ever right) they look right past the obviousness (they don't want to be simplistic either so they ignore anything that's too simple) and try to figure out an intricate and highly sophisticated truth in the illusion thereby only causing untold problems and confusion.

However, there is a light at the end of the tunnel (or corridor depending on your taste) and that light is just what we've been talking about (actually you've been reading, I've been writing; and we both should have been doing something else) here, which is Enquiry.

Now the opportunity you're being given if you finish this little gem of a spiritual masterpiece, and understand it, is far superior to the opportunities given to the modern man or woman by the traditional forms of Enquiry. The traditional forms were fine for their historical counterparts of the spiritual seeker (for their environments and cultures) but the new age devotee needs a form of Enquiry that is specifically suited to his mentality and to the form of the world in this troubled times.

And so at last, my story. There once was a dear friend who lived in our community and who had been out of work ever since he had begun to study with us. He therefore barely survived and was not at all able to support the community through any financial or material forms. He did, however, support us in other ways as he was a very quick witted fellow able to recover from shock in the fastest time I've ever seen it occur. So his recordbreaking feats of retreat into the mediocrity of maya kept us all in quite good humor generally and absolutely in stitches on quite a few occasions specifically. Well, one very fateful day he re-engaged a previous employment, which was that of a real estate salesman.

I had been trying for years to get him to understand Real Estate, which is another story altogether, and you know all about habits by now, eh?

So as I was saying (writing actually) he, being very good at his job, immediately sold a major estate and was going to collect about $6,000.000 (that's six thousand dollars) as his commission when the sale was finalized. He had always said that when (and frequently If, being both a practical realist and a hopeless dreamer) he got a job, or an inheritance, or any windfall that he would donate it all to the community.

As this reality was present about to become true, or stare him in the face as they say (whoever they are is a mystery but then that's what mystery schools are about, which is another story altogether, etc...) he began to seriously contemplate his previous fantasies (about $6,000.000 seriously). We were sitting together quietly sipping some excellent herb tea when he said, and I quote: "Who am I kidding to think that I'll give my commission to the community!" And he promptly left our company never to return again.

What is this world coming to? Since you ask, I'll tell you. Nothing it hasn't been for a long time already.

Anyhow, at the moment he said that statement (a series of words, or a phrase, or a sentence or partial sentence) I was struck with a mind-numbing, blinding flash of realization which, Thank God, I was able to remember long enough to write down. I realized that moment that his unconscious utterance could herald a new dawn for the spiritual seeker. A revelation broke through an otherwise dull day like a million suns shining in the heavens and illuminating the universe to its very edges.

I realized, being somewhat of a scholar (a poor fool who has mistaken knowledge for everything else) of the ancient spiritual traditions of mankind and womanhood that a new Enquiry was here at long last. I saw that the Enquiry for the modern world had been born and no longer would we have to rely on outdated and antiquated methodologies.

I saw that if one were to merely use the statement (a passage or group of interconnected words) "WHO AM I KIDDING?" and continue to use that Enquiry without surcease that one's True Nature would have to become known and one's destiny would be fulfilled as prescribed. The beauty of this incredible illuminating realization regarding "WHO AM I KIDDING?" is that this Enquiry can be used at any time, about any experience regarding any feeling or any thought that the usual man or woman will ever have. Neither intelligence nor discrimination are at all relevant.

Anyone may simply ask right this moment "WHO AM I KIDDING?" and when the answer becomes clear, VOILA!

WHAT CAN I SAY?

For The
Love
Of God

God cannot be attained, or sought, understood or bought. God cannot be "had" in any sense of the word, by any stretch of the imagination.

God may be lived. But how? Only through the most absolute, selfless, and totally sacrificial Love. God, in order to become truly "The Father" of Jesus, or "The Guest" as the sufis would say, must be loved beyond mind, beyond senses, beyond all that you see and all that you don't. Only Love absolute will do.

God does not appear to those who beg, who cringe, who seek for His Divine aid. Nothing must be asked of Your Lord. He is not the Beloved, the Very One, the Only Real, to one who asks of Him a favor. The seeker, wanting of the Very Lord validation of his or her maya, his or her illusion never realizes God in Truth. God is not the explainer of the dream. God is not the fulfiller of the wish. Of any wish that turns in upon the wisher. All prayers that reflect the prayer are not to God. Such a prayer is ego asking itself for some "goodie", some recognition perhaps. The prayer only reflects His Divine Glory. He is only Love. Any desire that turns in upon the one who desires that is not asked of God but of the separate one. All such involuted prayer is merely a self-meditation.

To see God face to face one must never see the face of personality, of "the wish". One must see only the face of God, as He gazes at His child, His lover, His only one. You must not even place yourself last if you are to see this God. He, that you have heard so much about and for whom you have longed and ached through eons of ages, through time uncountable and unknowable.

No, you cannot even put yourself last, for you still then have a self to be seen over and against the One, the Beloved. You must lose this stubborn little one. You must not even know "you" exist. You must not "put" yourself at all. There must be Only the Lord, the very Beloved of all ages, times, worlds known and unknown. There must be God.

You must love God above all, above family, friends, shelter and food. You must love this God whom you do not know in your heart so fiercely, so one-pointedly, so mindlessly that His grace, this most profound Gift comes to reside in your heart. The Guest, when He comes to visit, may remain or depart at His whim. You must prepare His alter, this house so that He finds it so beautiful, so to His liking, that He stays. He must be pleased and only the purest, most selfless Love, will please Him thus. This Love must be blind, deaf, dumb to all but Him. This Love must seethe with ardor and passion to please only Him, this most treasured Guest. This Love must at the same instant be cool and tranquil, at peace to the very core of the lover. The Beloved needs constantly to be shown the quiet strength of perfect devotion, Bhava. This special Guest, once He has accepted the hospitality of this humble home, will expect much of His host. Cleanliness, honor, integrity, trust - All of this to be lived. No dry philosophical argument will do. The armchair devotee will never, never do. The man, long on words, hort on action, is never able to entertain the Guest for long. The Lord prefers those who "DO". To those go His arrows of Love, of bliss His ecstacy is for His lovers, not His admirers. The joy of the Beloved is the joy of the Lover. The one who attempts to own Him is left only with sorrow, loneliness. The one who has forgotten what it is to own, whose mind has been lost to the Lord of all creation; such a one knows God's humor. Such a one laughs with this new found Friend, the Guest who has moved into his heart. The one whose peals of Divine laughter resound throughout the universe, this one nas lost his heart entirely. The Guest has assumed it, has taken it over, never to let it be apart from Him again.

But the Lord must be Loved. Loved with the entire being. He must be loved with all of such a one's body, brain, mind, emotions, senses, feelings. God must be loved to distraction. Totally and without cease. He demands your constant attention. He demands your life, for He will only make you His under those circumstances. He wants not the fine complimenter, the spiritual fop, the divine poppycock, the religious milquetoast. The Lord settles not for the meek of Love. Only those meek to the illusion of the world become His in Truth. Only those who love madly, as crazy men and women, only these attract the Guest. Only the Lover may justly invite the Beloved to spend the night. Only the Lover tastes of this Beloved's delights. The Lover comes to know His sweetness, and tastes the nectar of His lips. Only the Lover may feast his eyes upon the beauty of the Very Lord.

God, in his magnificence, almost too much for anyone to bear, shines forth to the Lover as His Beloved. At last He is here. You have sought, fought, prayed and begged. He has stayed away. He has even become more distant. You have suffered as if this deep primal loss could almost be touched. And it never can be, and you have cried.

At last you have decided to Love. The hardest thing in the world, in the cosmos to do. To Love. And that has become your only alternative, for all others have failed. It is easy to desire, to want, to use, to control, to manipulate. All so easy. It is even easy to hurt, to plead, to ache and to die. But to Love. To really Love. That is for no ordinary one. That is for the ones who must live God. It takes conviction, enough to face the tempests of the hells. It takes faith, enough to leap uncaring into the great unknown. Ah, to Love. And only this brings the Guest to your home. For He knows where He was born, and where someday He must return. He waits only for this sign, only for you to notice Him, in Truth at last.

This Beloved, our Lord, our God has waited for time

unremembered, for ages only vaguely intuited, for you. He waits to return home. You call Him a guest. Do you not know He has built the house? Ah, Lover, awake! Know Him, this one who has been so patient, who has waited only for you.

As Krishna's gopis danced at the mention of their Beloved's Name, as they fell ecstatic to the earth at the thought of Him, as they exploded in Light at the sight of His form, as they Loved Him, so, too, must you Love your Lord, your God. Love Him that He may take you, consume you, devour you. And His bliss will be yours. His peace is your very life. His humor, His happiness, your sun.

The Beloved waits still. Can you so dispassionately keep closed the doors of your soul? He waits for you to Love Him, that He may become the Guest once more, becoming your permanent companion, your friend, your life itself. He asks only that you live for Him, that you remember always Him, that you forget who you were, becoming lost in Him. Can you forsake this most earnest request? Nay, but just Love. Become the Beloved and Live!

May the Blessings of the Beloved, Allah our Lord, Shiva, Christ, Buddha, be patient for you.

"Thank you, Lord, for having once visited this poor one, staying. And, Father, this one must confess he has still one small desire left. He prays that you let him keep it. And this is to always remember You, Your Grace, with the gratitude that he does now. He rests in awe at your Gift, his head bowed before you, His Beloved. Amen."

*Dedicated to the
countless, infinite
number of devotees
who have unconsciously
and with no prior
knowledge fulfilled
this Path.*

The Divine Path
of Growing Old

The "Divine Path of Growing Old" is a totally new and absolutely significant form of spiritual practice never before known to man in it's true nature and potential.

Several highlights of this path are to be noted, and when clearly and concisely seen for What-They-Are, can be recognized as obviously placing this Path far superior to any other form of spiritual practice known to modern man.

Please note I say known to modern man, for certain very exclusive ancient cults had begun to pierce this Divine Path in their search for secret knowledge but even these never fulfilled their practice and as a result were left with only a partial picture of this always true and only perfect Whole. Now for the first time, as a result of a most lucid and amazing awakening of mine that I will shortly describe, is this Path made available in its totality and presented here to those fortunate enough to be reading this. This path has been completed in my case (psychically) and I have a full grasp of its mode of fulfillment so that I may teach it and bring others into its most mysterious and beneficient ecstasies.

One of the highlights earlier mentioned in this treatise can be seen thusly, please pay attention and follow closely my train (or bus if you will) of thought. If you will simply examine the written, oral, and visual history of the human race (not to mention the sub-human or beastial kingdom, which is another story entirely and will perhaps be elucidated and explained in full as this Way becomes more widely accepted and seen and the more esoteric sides of its Real possibilities are desired to be tasted) you will most readily become aware of the fact that everyone, without exception, ages. You may not think that this is very profound. However I beg your indulgence for a short while longer so that as I explain my most perfect insight into this "Divine Path of Growing Old", you will be enlightened to its most exceptional profundity.

So: Everyone ages. You may also feel that this is so obvious as to be ridiculous, but therein lies its beauty and in this mundane obviousness lies the very reason that the most wonderous "Divine Path of Growing Old" has never been seen in this light before. For God, in all His glory and with His somewhat perverse sense of humor has chosen to place His Most Perfect secrets in the most readily approached locations.

At any rate, the beauty of this obvious fact is that you are able to, within extremely well-defined limits, predict exactly how your practice of this "Divine Path of Growing Old" has begun, will progress, and ultimately will end. This knowledge that since everyone ends up dead and almost everyone ends up after death to be some sort of food (with the minor exceptions of those unlucky enough to be frozen stiff or preserved perfectly-as-if-alive, for whom this Path is ineffective in its ultimate end result and for the very reason that this Path should be a deterrent for such foolish and utterly childish behavior) when seen in its unavoidableness is a great comfort, a soothing companion as the Path is traversed, and all the security that any one really needs.

This most miraculous and sure to be highly controversial "Divine Path of Growing Old" came to me in the most natural and unpretentious surroundings. I was marveling at how successful a number of my friends, associates, and acquaintances were when only several years ago these very same people were the most derelict bunch of no-good, dirty, irresponsible, achingly poor clods one could never hope to know. And as my mind digested this seemingly impossible transformation that had occured, IT came to me in a mind numbing, thought shattering eternity of several seconds. I at last knew the sought for, killed for, martyred for secret of all life, all death, all existence, and all anti-existence. I had in the eternity measured on the second hand of the watch worn by one of the compatriots whom I was with at the time as two units, realized the "Divine Path of Growing Old".

Yes, I had seen that everything works so perfectly that we may follow this Path intelligently and achieve what the greatest traditions have eluded to and hoped for: Life-As-It-Is!

If this "Divine Path of Growing Old" is accepted and made our very own, and if our sadhana keeps us intent upon committing our lives to its completion and fulfillment we will see the most marvelous spiritual results.

We will see that our first several years (stage one of the "Divine Path of Growing Old") are parallel to the initial stages in other spiritual Ways. That is we are totally unconcious of anything relating to Real Life or God Realization. We are merely dummies. Now anyone with a mote of common sense can see that in Traditional Paths of the spiritual life this first stage is generally undertaken during the early twenties or later, and at times not even being begun until mid-age! Here, in the "Divine Path of Growing Old" this stage is already completed and fulfilled, painlessly and freely by the age of ten.

Stage two in this infinitely perfect Path also parallels the second stages in the traditional religious and spiritual forms of study. In stage two we feel that we know that we are always right, no matter what the circumstances. In the traditional forms of spiritual practices and other common paths, stage two usually remains forever and is only rarely transcended. Higher stages are usually assumed and acted out by the practitioner but in fact that is quite an unrealistic and stupid assumption. In the "Divine Path of Growing Old" however, as we approach stage three, we must, by the very weight and volume of evidence to the contrary see that stage two was a necessary part of our education but not a real, true, or permanent state. And so naturally, without any effort at all by our thirtieth year or so (which is why you may have heard it said, "Don't trust anyone over thirty) we automatically go on to stage three. In rare cases stage two lasts several years longer and in even rarer cases stage two lasts forever but since this is just the opposite of all the other spiritual paths we can immediately and with heartfelt assurance put our money on the "Divine Path of

Growing Old."

Stage three is called the mature stage of the "Divine Path of Growing Old". Here we begin to sense that there is more to life than our personal and individual (and quite often little, picayune and truly insignificant) world. And we bring our whole past experience of growing up to bear in our maturation and judgement. We begin to indulge such diverse forms of BEING as hero worship, power tripping, unbridled desire, neuroses, psychoses, psychosomatic everythings, transference, rich and wide-ranging fantasy, being-the-expert, and others much too numerous to list here.

This stage typically lasts for twenty years or so, again with occasional exceptions. In the more popular Paths that many of you be familiar with, stage three often seems to be active but the dynamics of stage two (always thinking one is right no matter what the circumstances) underlies and permeates all of the aforementioned qualities of BEING, therefore only approximating stage three but still being stage two. This can easily be seen by observing the justification of the practitioner as he/she explains his or her position on the ladder of attainment. This never occurs in the "Divine Path of Growing Old" due to the unavoidable consequences of practice of this Path (which will shortly become obvious if they haven't already). These consequences being much more relevant than even the superficial aspects of stage three. Loss of bearing, sagging coopers, erosion of the scalp and facial environments, and the almost universal Paunch.

Stage four of the "Divine Path of Growing Old" is the stage in which the key to the whole Path (aging) begins to be grasped and seen in its true light and inevitability. Slowly it dawns on the earnest practioner of this Path that their entire life's experience all led perfectly to their present form and state of consciousness and that the Powers-That-Be cannot even change this dynamic aspect of Life-As-It-Is, aging (not that they would want to for any reason whatsoever). In this fourth stage one realizes one of the most inspired and unimaginable facts (than is almost never seen in stage two or three) ever to be realized: That those who had always been called older and wiser were truly That. And specifically, the rare and precious gem and most central point and core of that very insight: One's Mother was right. In other words she really did know what she was talking about.

In this stage four, one realizes that in fact experience is the best teacher and one is quick to help those less fortunate (still struggling to reach fifty-five years of age or so) to recognize the truth of the aforementioned realization, just as that one was helped by stage four practiners years ago. This is where highly acclaimed statement "do unto others as they have done unto you" comes from.

In the common paths so widely practiced today, experience is reacted to jealously and without respect at all, ergo stage four is almost non-existent in any other Way.

The fifth stage of what you must by now see as the most excelled and transcendentally pure "Divine Path of Growing Old" is a return to the outer form of stage one, but with an inner strength and conviction (impossible in stage one) regarding the nature of this Path of Real Spiritual life due mainly to one incontroversible fact: We have grown old. The core of the Dharma (teaching), namely aging, has been seen to be true in our case and we bring this deep inner knowledge gleefully and arrogantly to and through stage five. This stage is mistakenly called "second childhood" by those ignorant of the magnificient perfection and spiritual reality of "The Divine Path of Growing Old". In this stage, what used to be called "going to grandmas" in stage one is now called "puttering around in the garden" or "getting ready for the grandchildren". Now are you beginning to see the undeniabless of my most graceful argument?

And now we must discuss what I hope you have been waiting for (and I hope you have not spoiled it by skipping ahead to read the end before its logical sequence in the chain of events could be impressed upon you by the interim bulk of the little manuscript) which is the culmination and spiritually perfect fulfillment of the glorious "Divine Path of Growing Old".

It is, reasonably enough, death. Now please don't laugh, throw your hands in the air, cough, throw up, or assume that something that seems so simple couldn't possible be THE most Real completion of any spiritual Way known to mankind. It might seem to you that any fool could recognize this possibility but let me further enlighten you as to its uniqueness.

In any other path that I know of (any other path without exception) and I assure you that I know of a multitude of those ones, if one dies unexpectedly or before that one's Sadhana or spiritual practices are brought to their utmost point or possibility, the outcome is at best: Good Karma and at worst, maintaining some form of "status quo", whatever that is. All paths have a promised end result that is not necessarily a natural outcome of the path, but rather an artificially designed, imagined, or implied goal or level of attainment that must be worked for and efforted at with intense one-pointedness. If one should die before this artifice is reached, this individual who has just died suffers great frustration and turmoil once they are safely on the other side. Occasionally this great frustration and turmoil is not seen during transit because the Whatever-It-Is-At-That-Point is too busy to notice that its process had been cruelly interrupted in the prime of youth or in the dusk of old age when just at the edge of completion of artificial goal that had been sought for say, many years. (Didn't you ever get the feeling that you were so close to something you could almost taste it if you only had . . .)

However, as you can most clearly and stunningly see, in the "Divine Path of Growing Old", if one should die at any time, at any age, in any stage, one has only realized the culmination of this Path anyway so the only possible outcome is the joy of completion and transcendence. For as anyone knows, the object of the culmination of any path is completion. So to briefly sum up, since the completion of the "Divine Path of Growing Old" is death, one may die at any point in one's practice and attention to Real

Spiritual Life and its possibilities as made available through the "Divine Path of Growing Old" and the path will be perfectly culminated at that time. It is therefore literally, physically, emotionally, mentally, astrally, and etherally impossible to interfere with or stop the perfect realization and culmination of the "Path" we call the "Divine Path of Growing Old". This most transcendental Path naturally and always completes itself with or without the willful intention and/or participation of the devotee of this Path. Perfect security can be yours in the knowledge that you cannot lose, that you must win, through the embracing and joyous practice of aging through the medium of the "Divine Path of Growing Old."

Bless you . . . The End.

Presented as a service to all who truly wish to live God as His Divine Being manifest on the planet Earth in the galaxy called Milky Way in the Universe Solex Five.

Mosquito and
the Windshield

We got in a car the other day and as we took off, there was this mosquito. Occasionally, insects are caught inside cars and this one was flying around the windshield right in front of me. As I noticed it, I realized that these kinds of insects may live only a day. I mean, their full life span is maybe one day. They're born, they mature, they either mate or not, and they die. I was thinking about that little insect realizing that at any rate, under any circumstances, when that kind of little insect is born, it's manifest destiny is to live its allotted twenty-four or thirty-six hours. That's what it's given and every particular form of insect is given from the beginning a particular manifest destiny. Some butterflies live three days after they come out of the cocoon. They live, they fly around, they sit on a flower and they mate and then they die, all in three days. Each level of species has got a particular manifest destiny.

We have a particular destiny as well and we're allotted a certain amount of time. We're allotted a year or ten years, fifty years, seventy years. The average time the human being lives these days is seventy to seventy-five years and our time to live our particular life has been lengthened over the years.

Back in the old days, depending on how old the days were, a human being's average life span was twenty-five or twenty-six years. I was reading a story about Pericles and the old Persians and there was one lady there who at twenty-one years old was considered an old woman, because at thirteen or fourteen, they were in the prime of their lives, married and having children, fulfilling their destinies in those days. And now that we've come thousands of years up to the present, maybe the average life span is seventy to seventy-five years. And each of us is allowed a particular destiny.

And within limits, the limits of that particular mosquito's destiny, it happened to find itself in my car, driving along down Rt. 80 completely unaware, of course, that it was driving down Rt. 80. The interesting thing about that insect was, I got the strong feeling that it didn't know whether it was fulfilling its destiny perfectly or not. That insect was just on the inside of the window, buzzing along from right to left, back again, right to left and back again. I got the very strong feeling that it expected that what it was doing was fulfilling its destiny.

Now an insect of that caliber doesn't have a tremendous capacity for intelligent comprehension, basically, its instincts were telling it to head in a certain direction, toward the sun, and that's the direction it kept going in. It wasn't smashing its head on the window or anything like human beings who get into certain circumstances do. When they can't get out, they smash their head on the wall, purposely to try to knock themselves out so they won't be conscious of what's going on. But this little insect wasn't trying to destroy itself, it was just buzzing against the window, blissfully unaware that its destiny was going to be fulfilled, that it was going to live and die to fulfill its entire destiny in this Toyota station wagon, in the midst of three adults and five children who were all screaming their brains out at one another, the children at the children, the adults at the children. And that's all that the mosquito would ever do. It wouldn't ever create, it wouldn't ever meet another one of its species, it wouldn't create progeny to carry on the race. This little bug was just blissfully unaware of the whole process. This bug was allotted its twenty-four hours and that was its destiny and it didn't know or it didn't see any difference in fulfilling its destiny by flying around a Toyota station wagon and trying to get out through a window that was four or five times as thick as the breadth or the length of its body. It didn't know the difference between that and between fulfilling its genetic destiny, which would be meeting with others of its kind and mating and if it was male or female or both, laying eggs, and then leaving the eggs to hatch and on to another generation of that particular species.

And it struck me that moment as I watched that little insect, that it was not fulfilling its God-given destiny but simply fulfilling its manifest destiny.

And human beings do exactly the same thing. We have a God-given destiny and we have a manifest destiny. The manifest destiny is given to us according to heredity, according to the stars and according to the law of accidents. We're allotted a particular amount of time on earth, and that's our manifest destiny. Our manifest destiny according to the stars, according to when we're born, what time we're born, and to whether our parents were addicted to dope or alcohol, or had syphilis is whether we live a week, or years and years and years. And we also have a God-given destiny.

Now, most of us are exactly like that little bug, beating its head against the window in that Toyota station wagon, because our territory and the space that we cover in the years of our lives are our Toyota station wagon, literally. The same window, just as thick, the same adults and five children, screaming their heads off at one another. It's exactly the same, except the three adults and five children take the role of boss, parent, spouse, enlistment officer, and we spend our entire manifest lives blissfully unaware that there is another destiny. We spend our lives literally locked into a pattern of no-win. That bug couldn't win, because the windows were all closed, and that bug was to live and die in that Toyota station wagon, unable to fulfill its God-given destiny. And we're the same way, locked into a pattern of no-win. We're absolutely blind and we habitually follow all the patterns that are given to us to follow, hereditarily like the insect.

The insect was flying in one direction, pointed to the sun. So it kept beating its head against the glass instead of going into space and flying around. It would not leave the window, because it was going towards the light. That was its sensual heredity, flying into the light just as a moth will fly into a flame. That insect was flying towards the light, unaware that it could have flown around the car a little while, and at least had a bit of freedom in its life. But nope.

It was going to fulfill its entire manifest destiny in a no-win, no-place, no-show situation.

People do exactly the same thing, flying around in our Toyota station wagons, which are the limits of our environment, our economic capacities, and our incredible limited degrees of what we use in terms of our talents, feelings, and our feeling, emotional and mental centers. We go and we follow everything that's been put in front of us from the beginning, automatically. And we respond blindly to stimuli. Even the highest emotions that most human beings ever feel, are simply automatic response mechanisms to stimuli in the environment. We're programmed to certain response mechanisms, even the higher things we feel like love, compassion, or generosity, are just blind responses.

We feel a tremendous amount of generosity to someone who's been good to us all our lives, but when we go into New York and we see someone who's just as good lying on the street bombed out of their minds, we "know" it's their fault. We aren't even going to chuck them a quarter. We say, "They could get up and get a job. No self-respecting human being would be caught down here in the Bowery like this." We have no compassion at all for people who are lying around with flies buzzing around their head, and who are drunk out of their brains all the time, begging for quarters. But we go to our family and we have cousins and aunts and uncles who are worse than the people on the Bowery could ever be and we have compassion for them. We think, "Oh, gosh, poor cousin Ron, he's got such a rough life and the poor guy has got a degree in Chemical Engineering and he's resigned to being a salesman and making only a paltry $12,500 a year, the poor guy, I really feel sorry for him."

Our reactions are gauged by stimuli that we've been trained to respond to. All of them. We're in a no-win, no-place, no-show situation, inside that Toyota station wagon, living out our manifest destiny and having very little possibility. The average human being never has the strength to recognize their God-given destiny. Well, our God-given destiny, very much like the destiny of that little insect, is to sacrifice ourselves for the race.

You know some insects, like praying mantices, literally sacrifice themselves for their race because after they mate, the female eats the male, claws and all, because the female needs sustenance with which to grow the eggs. So her body swells up and she gets thousands and thousands of little praying mantises, but she's got to eat to survive, so she eats the male. And he literally sacrifices himself for the sustaining and sustenance of his species. And then she lays the eggs in that little cocoon and come springtime, thousands of little praying mantises come pouring out and all good teachers get one for their classroom every year and watch them come pouring out and all the kiddies look at it. And the little mantises eat one another up until they get big enough to eat grasshoppers and crickets and Japanese beetles which are much too hard for the tiny praying mantises when they are just born to eat.

And human beings have God-given destiny as well, and the only chance that we have is if our situation is recognized by one with compassion who takes us consciously, opens the window, and throws us out. And once we're thrown out of the window and free of the Toyota, then we have the possibility of fulfilling our God-given destiny. Now, if that one takes us, and we're in the middle of Rt. 80 and he throws us out and there's a big truck behind us and we can't get out of the way in time, that's the end. We get sucked into the truck and burnt to smithereens and shot out as more pollution. Then we don't fulfill our God-given destiny anyway. If we're out of the Toyota, out of the environment that man has created, we at least have a possibility though.

Now once we've already been given that chance, what do we do then? Human beings are minimally more creative than that little mosquito, not a hell of a lot, but minimally more creative. So we have this God-given destiny and the only way to fulfill the God-given destiny is only granted by the Spiritual Master. He is the only one with enough compassion to pick this lowly insect, that the average human being would mash at a moment's notice, and chuck it out the window. So the Spiritual Master will even pull the car off to the side of the road and open the window and throw the insect out.

Now there are a few misdirected Buddhists running around the country, whose credo is ahimsa, non-violence. They'll see the little insect and go, "Oh, gosh, we must get him out," and they'll take a piece of paper or their hand and try to get the insect out and crush it, give it a traumatic experience, or cripple or maim it on the way out of the window. Well, the same thing takes place with ostensible Spiritual Masters. There are a number of folks around that call themselves Spiritual Masters who are so misdirected that they will try to open the window and get the devotee out, but will just cripple or maim or kill in the process. The chance with the true Spiritual Master is to be given the possibility to fulfill our God-given destiny. Otherwise, literally, we're just like the bug. We beat our heads against the Toyota, for the whole time, fifty, sixty, seventy years.

The windshield is survival, the right side of the car is happiness, the left side is security, the back window, believe it or not, is love. Because we're much more interested in survival, happiness, and security than we are in love. Love is on the bottom of the totem pole. When you fall in love you might think that love is on the top of the totem pole, but you're wrong. When the average adult falls in love, they're not falling in love, what they're doing is establishing a more secure form of survival, or a more concrete possibility for happiness within the dream. If you examine your average love affair and your friend's average love affair, the love affair that your parents have carried on for however many years your parents have carried on their love affair, you will notice that it is ordained along the principles of survival, not along the lines of equating one another's lives together in God, or giving one another the space to grow equally, or to fulfill whatever they need to fulfill. They average love affair is simply a matter of survival, security or happiness, and love's the back window. And since most insects just beat their heads on the windshield until they die, they never know the back window exists.

Occasionally, a little insect like that will never even get to either of the side windows. If it's a wasp, or a bumblebee, or a yellow jacket maybe it'll get to the side windows. Some of those mosquitoes never even get to the side windows, they fulfill their entire manifest destiny beating their heads on the windshield. And that's the way human beings are, never confronting more than survival. The sensitive human being, the being who achieves a little degree of understanding or religion, gets to either one of the side windows, security or happiness, but it's only the very, very, very, rare individual who gets to the back window, love. And even that individual is still in the Toyota, a no-win situation, still beating its head against the glass. And many insects on the way from one window to the next get killed by the inhabitants of the car, which in a human's case, are the public school system and the parochial school system. We had eight. Right, three adults, five children: public school system, parochial system, government, and the medical profession, the media, industry, family, material aspects of the world that we think will fulfill our desire mechanisms. We could build a good Dharma around that. The adults being the government, the family, and those things that fulfill our desire mechanisms and the rest being children.

So we spend our whole lives in the car, beating our heads against the windows in a no-win situation, fulfilling at best our manifest destiny. Any individual who goes to a good astrologer and gets their chart done, will say, "God, was he or she accurate." Why? Because we're fulfilling our manifest destiny.

Where did we get our manifest destiny from? From the stars and from genes. We're involved in fulfilling our manifest destiny, and all the factors we can recognize in terms of what we usually think of as paranormal, or supersensory will just prove to us conclusively, that we're simply fulfilling our manifest destiny. Astrology, numerology, palmistry, tarot, all of the forms of psychic readings amaze us with the accuracy of the readings, but why shouldn't they be accurate? We're just fulfilling our manifest destiny. Every single one of us is fulfilling our manifest destiny. So why shouldn't one form of this particular life be able to read the destiny of another form? Of course, they are able to. If you get a tarot reading, it will be very accurate. Where do you think you came from anyway? The psychic realms. That's what created your manifest destiny, karma, that's what created your manifest destiny.

So here we are, being given one chance, that the Spiritual Master gives us. Now, what do we do about fulfilling our God-given destiny? What is our God-given destiny? Our God-given destiny, in so many words, is sacrifice into the realm of the primacy of the Lord, living, unliving and inclusive of all that arises under all circumstances. The average individual, who gets involved in some kind of spirituality or some kind of religion, is interested predominantly in a higher form of one of those four windows. A higher form of survival, life after death, a higher form of happiness, nirvana, a higher form of security, either good karma or the grace of the Master and a higher form of love which is fourth chakra, and unconditional love of all of mankind and all of God's creatures. The average individual involved in that kind of process hasn't been given the chance even to fulfill their God-given destiny, but is still fulfilling their manifest destiny on a higher plane or on a higher level.

But to fulfill our God-given destiny, we have to give up every remnant of the tendency and the tension required to fulfill our manifest destiny. In order to fulfill our manifest destiny, it requires an incredible amount of tension, because we're always being bounced back and forth between the play of the tendency to fulfill the genetic manifest destiny, and the tendency to fulfill the programmed manifest destiny that begins from day one. So we have the genetic destiny and the destiny from the stars. Perhaps the best one from the stars is a tendency towards illness or a tendency towards health, or a tendency towards long life or tendency towards short life. Maybe our genetic destiny is a tendency towards a particular form of disease, or a particular form of health or whatever it might be. And there's a drive, a psycho-physical drive to fulfill that destiny, then we have our programmed manifest destiny, which is all of that stuff that comes in from the time that we're born. You must be successful, you must compete, you must be smart, attractive, secure, powerful, we must earn a certain amount of money, we must have a certain amount of relationships with people, we must be able to get along, have certain principles, certain morality, certain ethics. We can't spit at the table or pick our nose and put it under the chair. So, we have this programmed destiny, which is given us by our environment, our school system, parents and our peer groups. And we have this constant tension between one form of manifest destiny and another.

Some people have it a little easier because the destiny of programming runs along with the destiny of the stars. Sometimes a child is born into a home where the parents are very good much into self-improvement and ESP, so they have an astrology chart done right when the child is born and the chart says that this child has a tendency for music. So the parents take as their responsibility to give the child those particular opportunities, and because the child does have those tendencies, the opportunity to develop musical ability is offered and he becomes a very good musician. So, in some cases there's not as much tension between the program and the destiny of the stars. In other cases, it does take an incredible amount of energy to sustain the existing tension.

So, we go for forty, or fifty or sixty years and more and more tension is needed to sustain that conflict because the older we are, the closer we are to "not surviving". When we are fifteen years old and survival is the window we're beating our head against, so what? You are fifteen years old, young, and free. When we're thirty to thirty-five we're still a little young, a little less free. We have responsibilities now. Still we're pretty healthy, we're getting along, we haven't lost too much hair yet, not getting grey yet. When we get to be fifty-five to sixty and we're no closer to surviving than we were when we were fifteen, that tension starts to become infinitely greater and the older we get, the closer we are to not surviving. Ego says we've got to survive above all. And the older we get, the more obvious it gets that we're dying. We start losing our hair, our energy, our musculature. Then our breath starts to become a little short, we can't jog far, we can't do the asanas as well, we become a little stiff, our eyesight gets a little weak, our hearing gets a little weak. We start to get to be seventy-five to eighty years old, and it all starts to go. We know we're dying, the closer we get to not surviving, the greater the tension. The closer we get to dying, the closer we get to fulfilling the destiny of the stars but not fulfilling the desiny of ego.

So on one hand, we have a destiny that's getting closer and closer to being unfulfilled (survival) and on the other hand we have a destiny that's getting closer and closer to being fulfilled (death), and the tension between those two gets greater and greater and greater the older we get. By the time we're in our seventies we're literally getting torn apart by that tension. Now we only have one chance of eliminating that whole absurd spectrum, I mean that's a ridiculous pattern, and every one of us can sit here and think about what an absurd pattern that is and it doesn't make a damn bit of difference. Because we're still getting more deeply engrained and enmeshed in that whole pattern.

The only possibility we have is of obviating the whole thing, because that's the only way it gets done. You don't work on it a little bit at a time and maybe get good karma and work on it next time. You either obviate the whole process of the conflict of tensions, or you get reborn in another lifetime in another body, simply to fulfill that same destiny again. Why not? All the things you get reborn with come from the conflict of those two tensions. You think good karma comes from God? How absurd! Good karma is the result or the effect of the conflict of those two tensions, and no matter how much good karma we get or how good a birth we take, no matter how high we are when we're born, it's still a process of fulfilling manifest destiny. Always. Unless the whole spectrum of the conflict of those two tensions is obviated.

There's only one way to do that. Wake up. Wake up *and* fulfill the Law. Because just waking up is not good enough, as you can fall asleep again. Sacrifice is the Law. The only way to obviate that whole process of the conflict of those tensions is by fulfilling the Law of sacrifice in every moment from now on. From *every* moment from now on. Of course, we don't die in any case. The universe continues to evolve and we have only two possibilities. We can live out that conflict of tensions over and over again eternally which is purgatory, although it does get better because the universe is evolving. So conflict of those tensions becomes more conscious. Nevertheless, at the level of the vital, however more conscious the conflict of those tensions become, all life is still suffering, as Buddha said.

The other possibility is one of fulfilling Divine destiny. There are no other choices, and there aren't any other destinies, regardless of what appearances might indicate. There is manifest destiny and there is Divine destiny. One either fulfills manifest destiny or Divine destiny. It doesn't matter how high one is, it doesn't matter how centered one is, it doesn't matter how many times one has been rolfed. None of that is relevant.

Student: Damn!

Lee: You ought to say "damn" at fifty bucks an hours. Thirty rolfs, fifty bucks an hour, that's fifteen hundred dollars. That's a down payment on a Porsche. Anyway, it doesn't matter even though perhaps one is on higher and higher levels or on more subtle planes. It's still manifest destiny.

Not only does the human being have manifest destiny, so do spirits and angels. Spirits and angels have manifest destiny to the same degree that flesh and blood have manifest destiny. So you might even be lucky enough to become an angel, but if you don't fulfill Divine destiny, it doesn't matter, you will still be fulfilling manifest destiny, angel or not.

Student: Would manifest destiny be equal to karma?

Lee: Karma is only one factor of that manifest destiny.

Student: So there is the possibility of transcending karma within the range of manifest destiny.

Lee: A lot of yogis do that. A lot of yogis transcend karma and create their own destiny outside the law of karma, and yet it is still manifest destiny, it is not Divine destiny.

Student: So anything short of the Law is manifest destiny.

Lee: Yes. Anything short of the Law is manifest destiny. There is no partial fulfillment of Divine destiny and no partial fulfillment of manifest destiny. Now we can't hold a limited notion of what sacrifice means. It doesn't mean giving everything up necessarily, it doesn't mean being a P.L.P. That is what they used to say when I was about eleven years old. All the kids would come up and say P.L.P. (public leaning post) and they would stick their elbow in your back. It doesn't mean that you get to have everyone cry on your shoulder, and it doesn't mean that you get to be a receptical for everyone's bullshit. So you shouldn't put a limited ideology around sacrifice. God, the inclusive unlimited process of the Divine, is sacrifice, moment to moment. Every instance the Divine dies, and is recreated. The universe dies and is recreated. Every instance, it is a process of Sacrifice, Sacrifice, Sacrifice. There is no sustaining of what arises. It is sacrificed the instant it arises, and then it is sacrificed again, it arises and then it is sacrificed again, it arises and then it is sacrificed again. The individual, who is not really an individual, but who purports to be an individual, can become perfectly sympathetic with that process of sacrifice, arise, sacrifice, arise, sacrifice, arise. It does not mean that the form must be altered; everything Sacrifices. Everything Sacrifices and arises in its own form. Right this moment you are Sacrificing. You are dying every instant. And yet you are not changing. Not that anyone can tell.

So it doesn't mean that your form will change. You will Sacrifice and arise as the very same form. What is important is the process, the conscious process, and the blissful and ecstatic movement that is God being that process. Otherwise, all that there is is the tension of manifest destiny, karma and other bullshit.

Karma and highly developed mind control is what some of the Yogis have, versus the tension of programmed destiny, which is the illusion of separate self; independent existence, winning to avoid losing, dominating to avoid being dominated, survival. In order to fulfill Divine destiny, which is true ecstasy, or the Real, we must become sympathetic with or identified as that process of sacrifice. Moment to moment. Now it is possible for an individual to have a somewhat intuitive and relatively intelligent grasp of the processes that are arising and subsiding as the world and universe. The Spiritual Master can discourse relative to the law of Sacrifice, service, manifest versus Divine destiny, God, not God, and all of that bullshit. The Spiritual Master is quite frequently in the beginning stages of spiritual life discoursing with students relative to that particular process. The discoursing itself is not Sacrifice, and yet one can have a relatively fine intellectual grasp of the rhetoric, the Dharma. On the other hand, a grasp of the rhetoric and the Dharma can never be equated with the fulfillment of the Law. First there is pragmatic fulfillment of the Law, with a possible capacity to discourse relative to that Law. You can never describe that Law. You can never project that Law as it is. You can discourse relative to that Law.

The language and the ideology and the conceptual framework is simply a given factor relative to the paradoxical existence of manifest beings in the midst of the void. How can we possibly come to terms with the fact that we are all here, alive, speaking, communicating, looking at one another, breathing, thinking, feeling, in the midst of the void; in the midst of the Divine Process which is absolute extinction. How can we come to terms with the fact that we are here? I mean we are here. We can talk about philosophical ideology for years, without stopping, but the fact of the matter is that we are here. We can talk about the illusion of the mind, and that we are all not really here, that it's all a dream, but that is bullshit. It is not a dream because we are here. All you have to do is look around to realize that we are here. And it is real. We *are* here. If someone comes up to you and tells you that it is all a dream, have them lie down on the railroad tracks when a train is coming, and see how long they think it is a dream. Because it is obvious, inherently obvious that it is not a dream. We don't have to do anything to try and figure out that this a dream. It is inherently obvious that this is not a dream, because we are here.

What has arisen is this very process and this very world that is going on right now. How can we say that this doesn't exist? It's absurd to say that this doesn't exist. In fact, the philosophy that this doesn't exist is founded on the same old need to survive. If this doesn't exist, then there is less chance that we won't need to survive. And if this really doesn't exist, then there is no chance that we won't survive.

It is not some high spiritual process of reality that this doesn't exist. It is all bullshit. The whole thrust of religion to prove that this is just a dream is simply to better the odds that we aren't going to die. That is all it is, plain and simple. It is implicitly and inherently obvious that this is not a dream because we are here. Believe it or not, like it or not, we are here. How absurd to say that this is a dream, because everyone of us knows that this isn't a dream. Every one of us knows that we are here. What we don't know is who we are, but we know we're here. We know that this is real. What it is, who we are, we have no idea in the world. But we know that this is real.

What is necessary is to fulfill Divine destiny, which is the only thing that is inherently and naturally blissful, because everything else dies. And since everything else dies, the tension required to guard against dying and protect survival cannot allow bliss. It is impossible to allow happiness to be present when eighty percent of the energy of the individual is trying to sustain survival in the face of imminent death, every moment.

Look at the statistics. We can walk out of our door, and we can have an elephant fall on us. It is absolutely true. We can have an elephant fall on us. Because we live in the face of imminent death, all of our energy is directed towards designing some sort of strategy to avoid dying.

We're going to get frozen, so when the Fountain of Youth is discovered, they will un-freeze us, and we will drink from the Fountain of Youth and live forever. The only problem is what happens when there are no more generators to keep the freezers on.

So we're developing all sorts of strategies to avoid dying, when in fact, the process of the universe is extinction. And it is absolutely necessary to lead a full life of devotion to melt into that process, that Law that is Sacrifice in every moment. We can prepare ourselves for That, which is the most that a spiritual student can do. The Spiritual Master is the key or the benefit of devotees who have a conscious wish, or recognition of the need to fulfill Divine destiny.

At some point, we must understand the need to fulfill Divine destiny so that we are willing to submit to the Spiritual Master. Why, under any circumstances, would we walk into the face extinction? Why would we walk into the void? Why would we sit and bow our head to the ground in the face of literally nothing? We must consciously and intelligently realize the need for real spiritual life, which is Sacrifice, moment to moment. And we must be very sure not to put a definition on Sacrifice. We must simply fulfill the Law in order to live Truth, whatever that means. We can't say what that means like, "Yes, I'll never lie." How do you know? Maybe you'll be required to lie. We don't know what it means to live real spiritual life. We simply must do it, moment to moment. The Spiritual Master is our benefit, our only chance, and submission to the Law is the only recognizable form of fulfillment of Divine manifestation.

You know, it is like if the window is open in the car and if the insect senses the change in climate between the car and outside, as some insects do, he just might fly right out. Or some have to be helped out a little bit. Some, if you leave the window open long enough, will fly out on their own.

When a man or a woman crosses the path of the Godman, there

is a possibility given. Everybody is given the opportunity, everybody. And it strange how many people get a tremendous flash about the possibility of flying out the window but don't do it. They see the window open, they feel the difference in environment, but they won't fly out the window. Because it becomes such a habit to go in one direction that, even when a possibility is offered, they will keep bumping their head on the window.

So it is up to the individual. It is necessary for the individual at all times to make him or herself available in several ways. No matter how long we understand the preliminary aspects of the work, such as meditation, exercise, diet, if we don't recognize the need to live total sacrifice, we don't exercise our only chance. If we don't recognize the life of sublimation in God, or sacrificing moment to moment, then we keep a part of us closed off from the possibility of obviating manifest destiny. Sacrificing moment to moment seems to ego to be losing all grasp and the rhetoric says that we must lose ourselves. But isn't it worth losing ourselves to gain God? To gain the Lord? We do lose ourselves, we lose the separative individual when we melt into God. We lose the self-meditative individual. We lose the independent one, we absolutely do. When we surrender or submit ourselves to the Law of Sacrifice moment to moment, we lose who we think we are, who we have invested in , the personality, the individual, the one that must survive. We do lose that, but we gain all of it. We gain the Living Lord. Because we become literally identified with what is arising *as* God, moment to moment. The sacrifice and what is arising as God are instantaneous. We can't even separate the sacrifice from what is arising. So the Law is sacrifice, and what is recognized in the case of the devotee who sacrifices is ecstasy because we are identical with what is arising. That in itself is sacrificed every instant. We can't perceive the difference between the sacrifice and what is arising. So we lose all of what ego has built up or convinced us what we are. We gain what is arising moment to moment. We gain the Creator; we become the Living Lord, the sustainer of the worlds and the Benefactor of Love.

The Divine Way Of Falling Asleep

These days there is a very common malaise amongst the sophisticated spiritual seeker. It has been called various names from pantheism, all the way to "I Am That".

The hip philosophical statement to be heard ringing from the halls of academia to the steps of surburban ashramia revolves around this position of being already and presently enlightened (awake). That is, there is truly nothing (no-thing) to be attained. This absurd posturing that is so evident at all levels of the rank and file of the American spiritual populace involves the mental belief system surrounding a watered down and much bastardized Zeny (zany) or mahayanic concept.

The Western attempt at spirituality has abortively come upon what seems to be a philologically pure cop out, at once safe and secure, as well as, at least superficially*, Real.

Now, after all my linguini posturing; (oops, excuse me, I mean linguistic — well, you must admit they are close!) to the point.

It has dawned upon the logical and extremely well-trained (even enlightened) mind (mind you, I said mind, nothing else, just mind) that the search only brings suffering and eventual downfall and death, and is just an illusion at any rate, so a viable alternative has long been sought. At last the spiritual community at large has seen this somewhat presumptuous and often glib point that there is nothing to be attained, nowhere to go, no one to impress, etc...

The sophisticated spiritual seeker has seen in mind this beautiful airtight alibi for suffering that tells him (or her) that enlightenment is already perfectly present, full, rich, and gloriously alive in every individual's case. That awakening is

*which is enough to convince all but the most earnest and sincere ego anyway!

present now, not in some Edenic future or some other-worldly nirvana. After all, Buddha himself has told us so, and if we are attentive and perceptive enough, not to mention spiritually well-versed enough, we can find agreement in Jesus, Krishna, and even a whole shitload of contemporary (living even, they say) teachers as well who will all be the first to tell us (their students being the close seconds) that they personally are the fulfillment and culmination of all of the great masters and sages of the ages anyhow.

So we find ourselves in quite a dilemma. At least that's the way it seems to me. How is a real Teacher to communicate when the scene is filled with the most outrageous religious fops, even the most sophomoric of whom lays down this sensitive and sincere rap about we're all God and so is the sunset at dusk and the sunrise at dawn.

What can one do to convince the dedicated aspirant that all is not peaches and cream (how can it be when most of them are still celebate — get it?) and that this position of "nothing to be gained, attained, or feigned" is just another position? Is that even necessary? Let me attempt to answer that for you: No, not necessary, simply appropriate.

Don't you know (and you must if you've found your way this far into this priceless little gem of Truth) many, many people running around who swear that everything is perfectly attuned to God and that their lives are just functioning as smoothly as can be when it is clearly obvious to you that they could hardly be more fucked up.

Wouldn't you love to be able to help them (and you know every time you try they get quite indignant, letting you know unequivocally that *they* don't need help. Their life is perfect in God). Well, this is it: "The Divine Way of Falling Asleep", the perfect pill for the maladjusted (who is sure of how well adjusted he/she is) seeker.

When properly applied, and followed with dedication and discipline, this path will do exactly as it promises. The practitioner will fall asleep, thereby being able to at long last realize what is the case. Once the earnest seeker can honestly be responsible for what is, then he may truly begin Real Work which can, only when prefaced by stark honesty (which is not the case in all those presuming they are already awake because God is all there is), be the entry to Real Awakening or the realization that, in fact, there is nothing to be attained!

So, on to the Way. Stage one of "The Divine Way of Falling Asleep" is to realize that we want to really fall asleep and so commitment to this Way is a necessary evil. (Those who assume they are already presently enlightened generally find commitment to anything to be quite evil and tend to avoid it at all costs, even at the cost of Real Love or Spiritual Slavery.) We must begin to see that only constant inattention will fulfill the Way and that one or two hours a day (even the same time everyday) will never do. We must be attentive to inattention and lack of conceptual cognition at all times. We call this "self-forgetting". This stage one, or our self-forgetting stage, requires perhaps the most drastic hard labor on our part because it is the most foreign and offensive act to the ego (which has lead us to make the big mistake that got us into the pre-Way predicament in the first place). Self-forgetting simply requires of us, as we briefly mentioned before, *inattention*. We must stop seeing all that transpires in our lives with the great insightfulness we treasure. We must stop seeing our self (that which we seek to forget here in stage one of the Way) with such brilliant clarity and such transcending wisdom. We must stop seeing the meaning behind everything and understanding all and everyone. And last of all, we must give up all of the precious psychological concepts, determinations, and criticisms that we have gained and highly paid for in the struggle to become clear, centered, aware, and awake. All of that must be forgotten. We must simply begin to do what we do and live as we live and that can only be accomplished through self-forgetting. Once you have seen self-forgetting begin to become natural as a way of sadhana for you, we can move on to stage two.

Stage two of this "Divine Way of Falling Asleep" involves

realizing as we fall asleep that we might never wake up. We must come to see that there are an infinite number of possibilities that await us, or rather that may occur in the fulfillment of falling asleep and the most threatening of all of these myriads of possibilities is that we just might not wake up! We might stay asleep for the rest of our natural lives and just pass over (die) while still asleep. This stage is a little easier than stage one because since we've already begun to be mastered by self-forgetting, we find any fear of loss that may have ocurred prior to our entering this Way isn't present anymore. Once we have forgotten self, what is there to lose? So basically a heartfelt knowledge of this aforementioned possibility must be assumed and lived and at the same time we come to see it is OK if we don't wake up because sleep is usually quite peaceful and secure, not to mention unconscious. After all, you've all had the experience, I'm sure, of having some great calamity occur in the world, maybe even right next door to you, while you've slept and you've been blissfully unaware that there ever was a problem (until after you've awoken which you must have done at some point in order to be reading this, so don't deny it now). When you're asleep the world could crumble around you (which in fact of truth it is) and you wouldn't even know it (which in fact you don't). The only way you know the house down the block is on fire is when the sirens wake you and what a mess, all that noise and those lights and the fear of it happening to you someday. Wouldn't you much rather have slept through it all? Of course. And that proves my point.

So, to recap stage two of "The Divine Way of Falling Asleep". We must simply know and have it be perfectly OK (as OK as *any* other possibility) that we might not wake up for as many kalpas as there are grains of sand on the shores of Mother Ganga. Once we can live (or sleep) with that we can proceed.

Stage three is where the Way really begins to get interesting. Now we must actually go about falling asleep but we must know in stage three that we might possibly dream. So we must do two things in this stage: make preparations to sleep and if we have dreams, make the space to take care of them. The first part of stage three is relatively straightforward. We must find a comfortable place where we can fall asleep. We must pick an appropriate place because we don't want to fall asleep in the middle of the lecture, leaving our students in disarray, or even worse fall asleep in the middle of a bowl of hot soup, leaving our hosts in dismay and our face scolded and scarred for life. We also definitely don't want our beards full of egg drops or muenster cheese, which would be an awful blow to our vanity. Unless we were asleep, whereby we wouldn't care. There, you see, I prove my argument again. So we must choose our space with awareness, delicacy, intuition and a great deal of diplomacy. We won't mind being embarrassed or losing face ourselves (we'll be asleep, so it won't mean bobkes to us) but to those in our peer group who remain awake around us, our profound new sleep stage is liable to be not only offensive but highly embarrassing. It will be so offensive, in fact, they are liable to try to put us away. At best we'll be ostracized because a sleeping dunderhead who has self-forgotten certainly tolls a death knell to any party. So choose your space with deliberate thought (as much as you are able to muster after stage one and two anyhow) and compassion for your so-called friends and lovers.

Next we need to be prepared to dream and to be responsible for our dreams when and if they show up. We already know that we might never wake up and in that case, of course, our dreams are liable to become our reality (since a dream is almost always only seen as a dream upon waking up from it!) This is what we must prepare for. If by some fluke we do wake up, we'll see the whole dream world for what it is anyhow, so no need to make preparations for that event.

Now, about dreaming in the instance that we don't wake up. We need to somehow implant a trigger mechanism in our fateful mind that may be uncovered in the dream to signify that the dream is a dream so we don't fool ourselves back into the poor state of being we decided to leave when we embarked upon the incredible and soon-to-be renowned "Divine Way of Falling Asleep". (After all, who would want to believe he was awake even though he was in truth asleep? What a bummer of an illusion that one is!) We can call this trigger mechanism something foreign and unusual so it will really stick out when we stumble over it. We will call it, "Grande Olde Discipline." Grande Olde Discipline is most definitely unusual for the dreamer or the dream so when it pops up we will be able to grasp it and realize. Now be careful. Sometimes we may create a dream that we have Grande Olde Discipline when in fact, even this belief is still only a dream. In order to avoid this deadly error we have to be quite committed to this "Divine Way of Falling Asleep" and keep the fine edge that our constant practice and sadhana puts us on. We must know as we settle into our space for falling asleep that this trigger mechanism is so deeply implanted in our budding consciousness that it is prior to all of the possibilities of the dreams we may have (considering that we may never wake up) and therefore will outlast the dreams and eventually pop up and be recognized, thus allowing us to rest in the deep and secure knowledge that everything is still all right.

Now once we have fallen asleep and are either dreaming or just drifting in stage four sleep (no REM — just void) after we have been assured that Grande Olde Discipline is in fact true for us, it can be said of us that stage three has been completed. Stage three can be seen nearing its final stages during the aspect of hypnogogic imagery when our eyes do very funny things and our visions are particularly acute, specific and intense. Once this period has passed and we have lapsed into Real Sleep, stage three gives way to stage four of "The Divine Way of Falling Asleep".

In stage four, what happens is that we must wait (patience is a definite virtue here that you are all encouraged to cultivate simultaneous to your perfecting stages one and two of this Way) until the secret trigger mechanism, Grande Old Discipline, makes itself known to us through the dream, at which time we must spontaneously Self-Remember which will complete stage four of this "Divine Way of Falling Asleep". One thing to watch out for. We are liable to wake before the trigger mechanism is seen and grasped, in which case the dream will be seen for what it is, SelfRemembering becomes our conscious celebration and we most likely will not have the least idea what in the hell to do now (since we've been trained to function in sleep, not in wakefulness).

That means we have to work our tight little (or big) asses off to keep from being devoured. We will wind up celebrating that very act of work in the end anyhow because that's the law.

Oh well, what can you do? I highly encourage you to embark upon this great Way immediately, with gusto, verve and stick-toitiveness for it is your only hope. Pleasant dreams and remember "Grand Old Discipline".

How Not To Act
Superior When You
Really Are

A Guide For The Spiritual Aspirant

To begin with, I'd like to encourage you not to let the title of this charming little treatise fool you. It is, I assure you, perfectly serious. You and I both know, in the secret core of our mortal hearts, that we are, in fact, superior. "Superior to what or whom?" You may ask. I will get to that post haste. It is first necessary though to make sure that you read this invaluable guide (from one who has been there —went, saw, conquered) with the appropriate attitude. It is my hope that you will be able to read this exposition receptively and intelligently so that you can derive the optimum benefit possible. That is how it is designed, at any rate.

First, who or what are you superior to? We must be serious about this question because it is at the crux of a very tricky spiritual need without which any real life in God is totally impossible. And this little goodie, this need, is faith. One must have faith in order to prepare the ground of our being for the capacity to sustain and the ready availability to Grace. Grace is the moving force of the very Lord through which alone life in God and, in fact, any real spiritual life is possible.

Under normal circumstances, a human being, man or woman, will be born in the conventional way, their first communication with the external world being blasted by noise, pain, gross discomfort, glaring light and separation from their only food, thus suffering almost irreversible trauma as a result of this harsh and inhuman way most babies embark upon their earthly life. This same person will grow up in an environment overpowering in its use of force, violence, competitiveness and cruelty (mental and emotional), as programming and behavior modification tools to mold the, by now, automaton into the very ideal itself. This propagates the almost total lack of feeling and insensitivity developed in early childhood and seen in adulthood as the most obvious and unconcerned self-meditation and rampant narcissism imaginable. This condition leaves the average adult in a spiritually bankrupt and karmically abysmal state of affairs. In short, a painfully mortal and unspeakably dull existence.

The aforementioned average adult is so busy seeking the satisfaction of every whim or sensual pleasure with which to remedy this petty existence that he is too busy to see what is right under his nose. He is too busy hiding from the obvious to see the Real lucidly. He is too busy trying to escape into heaven to slow down long enough to learn what in fact Heaven is!

The average individual is plainly and simply a machine. He works automatically and reacts blindly to external and internal stimuli without the slightest intuition or awareness of what he or she is all about. To even use the word conscious in relation to such an individual is almost a sacrilege. Now after that venomous tirade we come to the point, or one of them anyhow.

Real Spiritual life cannot be a pastime or hobby. It is no idle affair. God is all there is. Living God already present, full and rich, is the only possible joy or happiness and is itself Truth. If God is not a priority, an **absolute** priority, life can be at best stagnant and illusory ("ignorance is bliss"), and at worst an all too real, miserable and seemingly eternal purgatory.

At the same time only the very rare, only the exceptional man or woman will attempt to become involved in this Real Spiritual life. Even though the average life is one of misery, seeking, and tension, to give this all up for the bliss of God requires strength and faith that seems ridiculous and unnecessary to the dulled out TV minds of the masses. Even stupor and pain is thought to be superior to Effort. So the average man refuses to Work, and dies complaining and bitter, but immobile to the end, thinking his absurd active non-involvement in Life and Work to be Doing.

Anyone sincerely involving himself in a genuine spiritual environment is first of all in the great minority of human individuals and, secondly, needs a deeply intelligent view of himself and his world and a great capacity for sensitivity and considerateness, allowing room in that world for other human individuals.

Notice please and pay attention to the fact that I said **geniune** spiritual environment. There is a ground swell of activity and involvement in so-called spiritual scenes these days. Meditation is the current fad and gurus are becoming the new heroes for the under thirty crowd (taking the place of presidents, generals, sadists and astronauts). The average scene is a superficial attempt at a traditional spiritual path, with no real juice or power. There are very few real spiritual schools around even though there is a gross proliferation of schools and teachers claiming to be genuinely spiritual.

Also please note that the second requirement for the serious (humorously, of course) spiritual student is the capacity to give space to someone other than himself. The average individual is so entirely bound up in himself (as the totality of anything of value) and so completely turned inward (away from relationship with the other one *as* himself) that no recognition of another being's life is possible. It takes a very honest man or woman and a great deal of integrity to allow someone else the space to exist also (as an equal in God's eyes which ultimately boils down to an equal in your eyes since the "other" God is so intangible that it will never work for you anyhow). Clear relationship, which is the fulfillment of human aspiration is impossible without the seeming other. Actually the other is an aspect of you, but that is yet to be known. You probably know it already intellectually but that doesn't count in the face of the living fire of the Lord. You may know one plus one equals two but when you aren't expecting twins and that's what you get, deal with one plus one then with your customary "cool".

God, in order to face himself, arose as conscious life, as *maya*, as the play, *lila*. The "as below, so above" (or vice versa depending on your understanding) plan is for a human to face a human in perfect relationship. This is in effect God facing himself in divine love.

Now back to the point, and I hope you haven't lost the train of thought what with all this rambling! Anyone openly responsible for this kind of life (lived in accord with the Law of sacrifice) is without a doubt superior. We may say that all others are dead, brilliantly acting zombies, and that only the geniune spiritual student is alive. That alone implies superiority. But now to the word superiority itself. We are discussing superiority not as meaning 'better than'. So superior is not a form of separation, the good versus the bad or them versus us. This superiority is simply a more optimum appropriateness in the face of the Lord, the Living God. And it is most assuredly more optimally appropriate to be alive in God, than to be dead, distracted in the world, identifying with maya (you are not your genitals, believe it or not!).

So there are most definitively superior human individuals. And we number ourselves amongst them (or we wouldn't have the necessary humor to indulge the fantasies of this Lee Lozowick character).

Now comes the intricacies of this treatise. How not to act superior even though, in fact, you are. For ego does not let go of its hold even when you are sincerely involved in geniune God-Life. Ego only is moved by the will of God after who you think you are is dissolved in the heat of God as the inclusive totality of all worlds and universes, known and unknown. So ego, or the moving force of all delusory thought and motivated activity (the activity of the Lord is not motivated, it spontaneously arises moment to moment), will continuously attempt to use whatever is at its command to reroute the individual from the life of dissolution in God to the life of distraction in maya (suffering).

Certainly being superior is an excellent post to command. So ego, as long as it can (which is quite awhile so be patient), will try to use this superiority as its form of narcissism rather than allowing the aspirant to fulfill God's will.

One must always be aware of what he is up to. One must observe the process or activity of this ego as it attempts (and it will not let up for an instant, with the random exception of the Graceful presence of the Lord's will) to continuously force its illusory demands which are in direct contrast (even though occasionally similar in form) to the movement of Grace.

Acting superior, the holier-than-thou attitude and the intellectual snobbery so apparent in the put down of the poor deluded machines, by the advanced spiritual student is not an appropriate form of relationship. This kind of egoic motivation does not fulfill the Law, sacrifice. And Real Spiritual life must fulfill this Law, not only in the grandiose and heroic forms (you know, the old martyrdom trip) but in all of the seemingly mundane ways. What seems to be so mundane to many spiritual aspirants is, in fact, the real guts and texture of True Spiritual life. The Law is most relevant in the day to day forms of life such as eating, working, social times with friends, sex, and in time spent with others among the spiritual group with whom you live. One need not be the President of a country or the head of the United Nations to fulfill the Law. One need simply remember not to cut off every car on the road while he or she is driving to a spiritual meeting and is late.

So *acting* superior is strictly an egoistic endeavor, whereas occasionally it is possible that *being* superior and being responsible for that may be known in relation to others as a Grace or as sacrifice itself.

The serious spiritual student who has made this life as God his or her total life commitment is, in fact, superior but must always be observing himself or herself. Thus if *acting* superior arises as the play of ego, it can be immediately (the acting not the factual existence) sacrificed, turned over to the Spiritual Master, to give space to the will of God, Grace, to fill life and consciousness. The student must always be seeing in Truth what he is up to, how ego tries to claim responsibility for the play instead of turning it over to God. When he or she catches himself or herself acting superior, seeing the separation of self from God in the form of comparison to others or criticism of other forms of lila, he or she must allow this gross activity to spend itself and allow for optimum appropriateness to arise in its place.

This must be freely permitted for this optimum appropriateness only arises spontaneously and randomly as a result of Grace, not through any form of efforting or desire or muscling techniques. It cannot be programmed or modified. It must be given up to the Lord.

How is this sacrifice made? It is not made, it is allowed. It is imperative for the spiritual student to pay attention, to be aware and to observe with objective and often critical clarity.

The movement of self needs to be seen in what it is doing. If is acting out of egoistic drives and needs, this must be undone through the Grace of the Godman. You must allow the will of God, the Tao, to move you. You must not manipulate, remedy, or interfere with the appropriate fulfillment of the Law, of the move to sacrifice as God.

So when acting superior arises and through your sensitivity and honesty in relationship to your sadhana you are able to observe this, you do not have to try to change it, you must simply do something else. You must not attempt to stop acting, you must be real as an alternative to this acting.

You should not allow ego to dominate. Rather, you can defuse it by acknowledging what it is up to, and being clear and responsible for the fact of ego's activity. Through that mode of sadhana or relationship you will begin to optimize the life of Truth as God and gradually the amount of time spent absorbed in the joy of fulfillment of the Law, lost in God, so to speak, will predominate.

This requires active involvement in the genuine spiritual

community and a deep and always moving commitment to the living Lord as the absolute priority of your life over family, friends, power, security, and exclusive personal pleasure seeking. Make God your all and you will understand the universes and the worlds untold of. The paradox of your superiority will be clear to you and you won't need to defend it or attack others who don't understand (as is the usual case with the so-called spiritual attainee). This is your destiny. You must fulfill the Law.

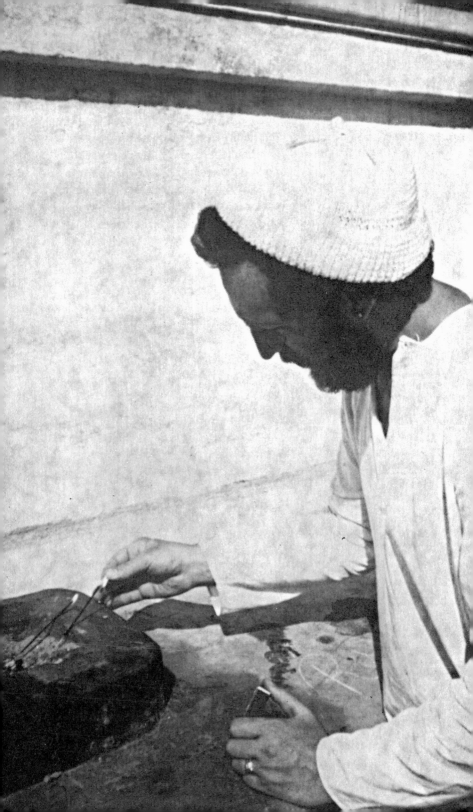

Meditation Techniques
For Self-Enlightenment

Before we can get into the real meat of things we first must discuss the actual subject of meditation a little. This is so we have a strong enough foundation from which to embark upon this journey that may well prove to be the very wellspring of our existence for the rest of our lives (natural and unnatural).

It is very important to understand the basics and the proper forms needed in this meditation of ours before we get on to the actual techniques. First things first, seems not only to be a tried and true old adage that warms the cockles of my heart but also a most logical and reasonable place to start.

And so we begin at "the meditation of the perineum". It seems like a "copper kettle full of sillyness" (as my grandpa used to say so often about everything except oatmeal with raisins and enemas) to begin in the fourth and fifth or sixth chakra when the lower ones are so hopelessly mired in shit. (As I always say about everything except God, Sex, and Food, in that order, the last two being a part of the first anyhow.)

The perineum is the physical part of the body between the front hole and the back hole, (which my mother was always saying to me when I was ten years old and always forgetting what perineum meant — which is why I kept asking and why my mother was always saying it) which corresponds to the first chakra of the subtle body of each and every human being. Once we can fulfill and perfect this "meditation of the perineum" we can then move onto more advanced techniques and higher levels of ecstasies.

Now, since you know where the perineum is you will close your eyes and gently (these very special techniques should never be harsh, ragged, or forced) and slowly rest in the quiet depth of your inner being. Let your attention rest on the perineum (not on either hole on either side of this "seat of consciousness at the base of the serpent's vertical tunnel"). Let your mind know that this is the first level that must be purified and without knowing what that purification is (which might only be partial and therefore a hinderance) know and affirm that this meditation will be perfected in your case. Know it will be so and it will be so. Continue to meditate exactly this way until your experience tells you that in fact it is complete (as your experience will tell you).

Once this most unique and extremely efficacious meditation is ripe and mature in your case, we move on to level number two. Now level number two has to do with the genital area so it is especially important for this one to culminate in its perfect richness before higher levels can even be considered, let alone attempted. You may find as your meditate that you feel a tingling, a warmth, a moist sensation, or even a feeling as if a great movement is arising in your case (particularly common in the male of the species). This is normal (you bet your sweet ass), (pardon me, I just lost control for a moment) so don't be disturbed or upset. If you allow this feeling to persist and continue along its own natural path of activity you may even find a divine pool of nectar has miraculously manifested after the stars, stripes, and lights of this natural progression have shaken your body and in fact your very being to its core. At any rate all of that nonsense is merely icing on the cake. On to the meditation itself.

You will again sit quietly, having previously perfected the "meditation of the perineum", and concentrate on the second subtle or psychic level. You will allow your consciousness to see what you are up to in relationship to this level and when you can take-it-or-leave-it as the very texture and stuff of your life (it may sound implausable, nay impossible even, but take it from me, it ain't) you may move on to level three.

The meditation of level three, the power center of the human animal is relatively straightforward but don't let it fool you. It is extremely hard to pull off even though deceptively simply. This fine meditation is to be done at the outer level with your eyes fully open and the mind and senses one pointed and totally aware, conscious, and centered. You are to walk into a singles bar with your foxiest or slickest outfit and you are to pick out the most attractive person in the whole damn place of the opposite or of the same sex, who is already spoken for (this may seem like a minor point but it is the crux and Real stuff of the whole meditation of level three) and you are to act like you are God's gift to the world of human animals and you are to make the loudest, brashest, and most outspoken public display and play for that person (the spokee, not the spoker) that you have ever done in your life. If this act of incredulous and beyond the call of duty act of bravery — yes, bravery, (you might have been tempted to say insanity but let me again assure you that bravery is the appropriate word here) is completed with no tics, tears, quivers, sweats, or cracks in the voice, you know that you are now advanced enough in your spiritual practices to move on to the next level of attainment. One last aside on this meditation of level number three. If you have diarrhea before or after this meditation number three, it ruins the whole thing (not to mention your clothing) and you must continue to practice it until it is letter perfect, or until you have no teeth left, whichever comes first. An added thought: what happens by the way, after you "play" may make you either reconsider what you feel to be the completion of level two (you may in fact spontaneously relive the level two meditation that very evening) or you may consider leaving spiritual life altogether. Note that these are only possibilities and please to remember the spiritual path to self-enlightenment is a long and hard road so Don't Give Up.

And now, once the lower three chakras (the basest level of all of homosapiens' blind animal tendencies) are "well done (baked at 400° until bubbly hot and steaming) we can get into something a little cultured for a change. Level four, the universal *Love* level begins to initiate us into the finer aspects of Real-Spiritual-Life as it has been traditionally known. Our level four meditation is associated with the heart. We all know that the heart means love and cards from Valentines Day, but what we will learn from our meditation of level four is about universal *Love*. In this meditation you will again sit quietly in a comfortable position (pick a time when you will not be disturbed or lock the bathroom door, the bathroom being an excellent place to meditate due to the vibes there of intensity, desire, and hard work, so no one will surprise you by accident) and let your awareness come to the center of your chest. As you do this regularly and with discipline you will begin to feel a hole (whole) opening psychically in your chest there. At first it will be just a pinpoint but as your meditation progresses it will become larger and larger. As this happens you will undoubtedly notice that there is nothing in the hole, that it is bottomless, and dark, and scarey, and spooky, and "MOMMY", No. . .back to being serious. As the hole gets larger you will eventually (if you stick with spiritual life long enough) find that as you close your eyes there will only be a hole (whole). No body, no mind, no nuttin'. You will also find that as you allow this void to become your entire being, that soon thereafter with your eyes open you will experience the same awareness. Notice that this does not mean that your life is bankrupt, rather just the opposite. You have now, at long last, struck it rich (spiritually that is).

As this hole (whole) continues to be present during all aspects of your Sadhana, you will lose all distinction of you-world-them-us, and in fact everything else and nothing else too. All distinctions will be lost and you will simply be void. Not null and void, simply void. Obviously, this state obviates the need for any additional meditation (since you, at this point can't even remember what your name used to be, meditation is the farthest thing from your mind, besides getting dressed that is). Therefore, the meditations of levels five, six, and seven become automatically negated and useless. Rubber pants or diapers become more relevant than Nirvana at this point. At any rate since you can not possibly hope to end your miserable separative existence by waking up, this completion of our level four meditation is certainly a desirable state for least your have become numb and blank which is certainly more desirable (as I just before) than realizing that; as Buddha said, "All life is suffering". God, what a bummer that insight is. So actually (as you may already have guessed, you sneaky little devil, you) these meditations - for self-enlightenment are really a perfect escape from the Good-Old-Rat-Race, but if that is how we had presented them to begin with you never would have read this, only to be spared the option of totally copping out — that at least now is within your very real grasp and possible experience. And now, the choice is yours. **To do or not to do, that is the answer."** Good luck.

Bless You

The
Ultimate
Play

Act I, Scene 1

(Scene 1: "The Ultimate Play consists of many players enacting a continuous narration. All words are spoken by a strong voice from an unknown narrator. As the play opens a voice is heard to introduce you to the "The Ultimate Play". The stage remains dark, jet black. As the narrator comes to the word "accident", a single beam of light and walking or moving through that beam are a variety of people, each dressed in a different, bright color and each making a different sound on various instruments. This continues to end.)

"In the beginning there was God. Only God. There was absolutely nothing (no-thing) else.

Then God had an accident. And then there was god. Not-only god. Then there was absolutely everything else. And it was good (accidentally). And there hasn't been an accident since. Ever. Not even one."

Act II, Scene 1

(Setting: All varieties of rock and metal (natural and man-made) surround the center stage where as the scene ends is exploded in a blast of flame shooting out of the center of a vast and deep pool of shimmering blue water.)

"Since god was brand new, and had happened all at once, like all babies he needed to learn about himself. So he figured he would start by learning about one extremity at a time — so as not to miss anything. He started completely at random, since one extremity was just the same to god as any other.

God, by the way, in case you hadn't noticed, had been completely forgotten by "now".

So god picked inanimate matter (leg) to know first. And there was gas, and there was rock and metal, and there was water. And there was fire. And then god knew these. And then he rested."

Act II, Scene 2

(Setting: Every corner and niche of the stage is covered by all sorts and variety of plants (real, no artificial ones) and flowers and in center stage, several of the cast dressed in green, yellow, and brown, moving to the choreographed dance number.)

"And so god decided to examine another extremity. And since they were all the same to him, he picked at random again.

And god decided to know flora (leg). And god knew flora from one cell to millions. Tiny flora in the water and in the air. Simple flora. And more complicated flora growing tall up into the clouds, and growing wide all over the face of the earth and the rock. And colorful flora, greens, reds, yellows, blues, and all combinatiions of those, more numerous than god had ever seen before.

And all of this took god much less time to know than the first extremity. For as he learned he came to know how to learn better and more efficiently as well.

And god felt invigorated by all of this glorious knowledge. He did not feel at all tired.

So he immediately went to the next extremity, at random again."

Act II, Scene 3

(Setting: Again every nook and side of the stage covered with animals (all alive, either in cages or flying and crawling and running every which way across the stage). With them move the cast choreographing the symbolic relationships that the mind has to various of the animal kingdom.)

"And so he chose to know fauna (arm). And he was overjoyed as he saw himself in so many forms, and with such vigor, strength and power. And he knew the amoeba and protozoa. He knew the insect and the fish. He knew the bird, the reptile, and the amphibian. And at last he knew the mammal.

He knew so much more now. He knew of flight, of love, of protection, and of parental pride.

He knew the sensuousness of the panther, the glory of the elephant, the fun of the otter, the love of the seal for it's young. He knew the wisdom of the cat, the industriousness of the ant, the freedom of the stallion on the run. He knew the age of the tortoise, the change of the caterpillar, the birth of the new, the death of the old. And he knew more, so much more.

And he was learning so quickly now. Everything was so wonderfully exciting. And in a long moment, it almost seemed like a dream, he knew fauna.

And he moved on.

Act II, Scene 4

(Setting: Naked cast moving through first the mime of Adam and Eve and the discovery of one another's nudity, then slowly dressing, one item at a time all the way up to being fully clothed in all manner of raiments including coat, overcoat, scarf, hat, etc... Throughout the dressing scene all the various emotions and sensations will be mimed.) "And now he came to Homo Sapiens, to man and woman (the other arm).

And he was amazed, he was ecstatic. He was very, very pleased.

And he knew things he had never known before. And he knew shame. He knew Adam and he knew Eve.

He knew jealousy, he knew so many new emotions. He knew pain as he had never know it before. He knew greed, he knew hate, he knew vindictiveness and revenge.

And he knew lust, he knew passion, he knew heartache.

And he knew friendship and joy. He knew possessiveness. And he knew elation, he knew depression. He knew pleasures, he knew lonliness. He knew joyous fullness, he knew boredom. He knew desire, he knew longing, and he knew the thrill of accomplishment.

He knew fear.

And he knew separation.

And he knew Mind (head).

And in the blink of an eye, he knew mankind,

And then he moved on, once again."

Act III, Scene 1

(Setting: Each of the great Ones named by the narrator will be individually portrayed from the time of their advent unto death. Men may portray women, women may portray men, and will in some but not all cases. Music crescendo's to a peak of orgiastic fury as the last word in the scene is spoken.)

"And this time, he chose, much to his subsequent surprise, to know something very different. For he had stumbled on the legs, stumbled on the arms and the head.

And now he had come to the heart, and had chosen to know this. And in a timeless, breathless, gloriously ecstatic flash: He knew Grace.

And what a discovery This was!

He knew Zoraster, He knew Krishna, He knew Moses, He knew Buddha, He knew the Nazarene, Jesus the Christ.

He knew Nanak, He knew Kabir, He knew Rumi, He knew Shankara.

He knew Ramakrishna, He knew Emerson and Thoreau, He knew Luther, He knew Francis, Therese, Seraphim and John.

He knew Gandhi, He knew King, He knew Meher Baba, He knew Maharshi.

And he knew so many, many others, countless, ageless, wise and free.

And for a moment, He was stunned. For a moment He was awed. For a moment He shed a tear. For a moment He knew Love."

Act IV, Scene 1

(Setting: The cast will mime all of the destructive events and qualities experienced by individuals — much noise and screaming — much dust, garbage, blood, and medicine all pouring into a large vat on the right center stage.)

"And he realized he hadn't much time. He saw that he had known what there was to know. He saw that the head ruled all of the other extremities. He saw that head could never know what He knew. But it thought it could. And he saw demise. And he couldn't quite believe it was real. So he made a game of it. And he loved games. So he **Played!**

He smoked. He drank. He ate everything he could eat. And somethings he couldn't.

He had ulcers, TB, cancer in such a glorious variety of ways, shapes and styles. He had migraines, and acid indigestion, and acne and heartburn. He had hardening of the arteries, colitus, angina pectoris, and strokes. He had massive coronaries and hemmoraghes.

He had apendectomies, laryngectomies, tonsilectomies, and hysterectomies.

And still he cried for more."

Act IV, Scene 2

(Setting: The acting out of the narrated action, as film of spliced parts of violent and destructive scenes from old movies (color only) plays on a screen to the rear of the stage.)

"He loved the game so much he played harder. He brought in friends to play.

He played arson and claim jumping. He played intrigue with a glint in his eye — lying and spying till all hours of the night. He had a special favorite, slavetrading. He sold women and enemies and moved up to Indians and blacks. What a smashing time he was having.

He played incest and adultery, blackmail and burglary. He played assault with a deadly weapon, and rape when that one got dull. He played embezzlement (just when he needed the rest). And he played murder and general all-around mayhem. He played crusades and slaughter in the name of the law. And burnings and torture to liven things up. And he was having so much fun he didn't want to stop. So he didn't!"

Act IV, Scene 3

(Setting: Each of the narrated conflicts acted out by the full cast with the back stage a scoreboard with two scorekeepers and a score for each conflict (the scorekeepers both costumed as angels).

"And his friends loved it so much they formed teams to play better.

And they played Athens and Sparta, and England and France, Spain and Mexico, America and Cuba. And they played Holland and South Africa, U.S. and Korea, Austria and Prussia, and China and Russia.

And they played the Boxer rebellion, and the War between the States, and the war of non-violence, and the Bastille day in France.

And they played championships!

The first one was glorious, with Germany almost outfoxing the rest of Europe and Russia, but America turned out to be the ace up the sleeve.

So they wanted a rematch. Fair enough! This time they got Italy and Japan to help. And they were about to tie up the score when lo and behold: America came to the surprise rescue again. With a magic mushroom and a grand slam, they made the score 2 and 0."

Act V, Scene 1

(Setting: The cast entering stage left with agonizing expressions and a myriad of aches, pains, bandages, crutches, et. al. and passing through an informal classroom in center stage furnished with a couch, large pillows, electric jolting rods, and hypnosis gear and a tub of water, a wet suit, and other "new age growth and consciousness movement" paraphernalia. Each of the cast will approach one of the center stage items, touch it or interreact in some way and leave the stage with an ecstatic expression. Back of center stage (at the rear of the classroom) will stand several "leaders either in three piece gray tweed suits and goatees or open shirts, beads, and white shoes, all gloating and leering — all with paper money one to two feet deep at their feet and a sun above their heads.)

"But some of the teams started to get tired of the same old games so they decided to invent a new one.

And after much though and deliberation they decided to call it "awareness".

And they played "you tell me your dream and I'll tell you mine". They played "the couch" (in three times a week installments lasting seven years — you lose if it takes less). They played encounter and sensitivity. They played mind control and biofeedback and this method and that course and then they played this path and that one and this yoga and that. And once again it was good.

And they played and played and played."

The Final Act, Final Scene

(Setting: All of the previous scenes and scenery piled randomly on the stage, and upon the narration of the last line, complete, jet black darkness once again.)

"And god began to find something very disquieting happening. Something vaguely yet surely discomforting. He started to know that the games he was playing so intensely could only lead to one place.

He saw that there was nothing else he could know. He had known his heart and knew that was the height that his knowledge could reach and he had forgotten it. He had regressed. And he began to see that he continued to regress and the only place that could lead to was his destruction. He began to know that the games he had been one playing for the last fraction of an instant were all unreal. They didn't work. No one ever won. Everyone just kept losing. He saw that his head had infected the rest of his extremities and was eating his whole body up. And when his body was eaten up he would be no more.

And he knew a new sensation. He knew a fear that he had never known before. It was deep, it was raw. It was broad and encompassing.

He knew that there had only ever been one accident. And this was all perfect. All appropriate. All exactly right. He knew that all of this was no accident. That it was all going exactly according to plan. And that was the scariest part of it.

There was nothing that could save him. He was a perfectly running, immaculately designed machine headed for his own self-designed obsolescence. And it was no accident. For there had only ever been one accident. And that was timeless ages ago. Ever since that one it had all been perfect. Perfect. Perfectly perfect. Flawless and pure.

So he lay down to await the inevitable. And he prayed to what he really didn't know although he had some very faint, very distant intuition of something to pray to. So he just prayed.

But god knew it wouldn't do any good because he KNEW. He had truly seen it. It was all perfect.

And he awaited his death calmly, patiently, unreservedly. For it was fate, inevitable destiny.

And in less than a fraction of a moment, in less time than any of his other knowledge took to learn, he appeared on the verge of doom. Right at the very edge. The next instant would be total darkness, destruction, nothingness.

And the second accident occurred."

THE END

The Student
And The Toad

It was about 3:00 in the morning a few nights ago and the dog had to go out. So I got up and walked all the way down the stairs, and took her out on the leash. And as we were going out to her favorite pooping place, there was a big toad, and he was just sitting where the rain pipe drains. He was having a good time, soaking up some water. So the dog passes by, and having never seen a toad before, really got hepped up. Of course, the first thing she did was put her mouth on the toad and take a big lick. And that was about all she needed. I pulled her away, since I didn't want her to chew him up, and as we walked down to the garage, she was spitting and shaking her head and sticking her tongue out, trying to get the awful taste of the toad out of her mouth. The whole time out there, she was whipping her tongue around because the toad didn't taste very good and she was trying to eliminate that negative sensation.

And it really brought sadhana to mind because for the traditional person who joins a spiritual community, this is a perfect anology. When he finds the toad, he initially does the same thing. He says, "Oh, far out," just like the dog who sensed life and that it was new. It was an adventure; it was exciting.

When the typical student finds something new, he thinks it could be an adventure, and he gets very excited. And upon first glance, it seems really far out. He senses that life is there and it appears to be a pretty interesting little event with some intriquing possibilities. And so he grabs the toad.

The problem with most people in spiritual communities is that they don't know to let go of the toad after they have gotten a taste of it. The typical person who is looking for God, so to speak, takes the "toad" in his mouth, but even though it tastes awful, keeps it in and even tries to swallow it. He just sits there with the toad in his mouth, and thinks what a horrible thing it is, instead of spitting the toad out, getting a drink of orange juice, and getting the toad taste out of his mouth. And the toad is maya — the illusion that, in our ignorance, we assume to be real or valid expressions of the Living Lord.

Of course, most people who are looking for God never even get that far. Most of them don't even taste the toad. The average person involved in spiritual life may see the toad and stand around and say, "Look at that! A toad! I wonder what it tastes like. I wonder what it feels like." But they will never actually investigate. People involved in real spiritual life will at least take the toad in their mouth, for it will look pretty inviting to begin with. But when the student gets to a certain point, he was to know when to keep investigating, and when to spit the toad out. When he realizes that it is not something he can chew on and get a nice taste in his mouth, he needs to spit the toad out and go about replacing the taste, one way or another. So if you are a dog, you go out and chew some grass, or you drink some water. Or because dogs sweat from their tongues, they run around and get all sweaty and get the taste off. You have to know when to do that.

There is a tendency for the student to grab the toad and say, "Well, at least I've got the toad. I'm not going to let it go". Getting the food is a really big accomplishment. It's our "investment". Most people look at the toad and remain dreamy or immersed in fantasy.

So when you get to that stage where you take the toad in your mouth, then what you must decide is when to spit the toad out and rinse your mouth, or when to chew it up and eat it. Even with frogs, you don't want to eat them raw. They are quite tasty if you can get some nice big meaty bull frogs' legs and cook them right. But you don't want to take a slimy, greasy old frog out of the swamp and just chew on it that way.

Sometimes when you come across something pertinent to sadhana, you need to work with it a little bit, you need to put it in its proper perspective. And sometimes, you just need to spit it out. But most students say, "I've got the toad, and I'm not going to spit it out no matter what, because I've got it." People are very obstinate. Even if they are doing something wrong, even if it is over and done with, they just don't want to let go of it. It is just incredible.